Richard Humphreys is a partner in Blake Morgan's banking and finance team. He has specialised in finance industry work for more than 25 years, and has particular experience in advising equipment finance lessors and motor vehicle financiers.

Essential Motor Finance Law for the Busy Practitioner

Essential Motor Finance Law for the Busy Practitioner

Richard Humphreys
Solicitor
Motor Finance Law

Law Brief Publishing

Published 2019 by Law Brief Publishing, an imprint of Law Brief Publishing Ltd
30 The Parks
Minehead
Somerset
TA24 8BT

www.lawbriefpublishing.com

Paperback: 978-1-912687-00-8

PREFACE

Without wanting to limit my audience, I should make it clear that this book is not aimed at the experienced motor finance lawyer. My experiences in giving training seminars on the subject have convinced me that many within the motor finance industry can struggle to see the wood for the trees. Those who are new to the area tend to learn things 'on the job', usually from those who have spent many years doing much the same. As a result, whilst many who work for the specialist finance companies have a broad and detailed knowledge which would put their external legal advisors to shame, others' knowledge is incomplete and lacking an overall understanding of the way in which some of the legal issues interact.

In addition, many lawyers who don't specialise in the area nevertheless need to dive into its complexities on occasion; usually on behalf of a finance customer with a problem. Such lawyers do not lack either ability or access to detailed legal resources, but can find it tricky to navigate those complexities in a cost effective manner.

This book is not intended to provide all the answers. It is deliberately brief, and some of the more complex issues have inevitably been simplified in the interests of brevity. The intention is to provide an overview; a roadmap which will allow those with less than 25 years' experience in the area a chance to approach the legal issues they encounter in a sensible manner. This approach may be related to a specific situation, or merely part of gaining a better understanding of the industry and its workings. In either case, I hope it will provide some guidance.

All law is believed to be up to date and correct as at 3rd December 2018, and all errors are mine alone. Without mentioning individuals by name, I would like to thank many of those within the industry that I have worked with and for over the years, who have indirectly contributed so much to this book. Finally, I should pay tribute to my family for putting up with me during the process of composition.

Richard Humphreys
December 2018

PREFACE

CONTENTS

CHAPTER ONE
INTRODUCTION

Some areas of legal practice are relatively self-contained, with most, if not all of the law required in order to deal with that area being easily locatable. Other areas, such as motor finance, are harder to get to grips with. Different sections of law overlap in respect of any given transaction, and as will be seen, which version of the law applies to that transaction can vary depending on the identity of the Customer. This often engenders confusion for those who are unused to the area. As a result, understanding motor finance transactions and dealing with the issues which commonly arise often involves peeling away the overlapping layers so they can be separately examined. Once each element can be understood in isolation, it is then possible to consider how they interact in any given set of circumstances.

One important aspect to grasp from the beginning is that a motor vehicle finance 'transaction' will usually involve three parties. For consistency, these parties will be referred to in this book as:

- The Customer – the company or individual wishing to obtain the use and/or ownership of a motor vehicle;
- The Finance Company – the organisation which is in business to offer Customers a range of alternatives to the outright cash purchase of that vehicle; and
- The Seller – the organisation which will, in practice, begin each transaction by selling the vehicle, usually to the Finance Company, but sometimes directly to the Customer.

Large sections of the motor finance market involve only these parties. However, mention must also be made of two other 'parties' who may be directly or indirectly involved in any given transaction:

- Brokers – intermediaries who operate to bring Customers, Finance Companies and Sellers together and/or otherwise arrange transactions between the three; and

- Regulators – statutory bodies which oversee aspects of the motor finance market and exercise varying levels of control over many transactions.

The intention of this book is to take the reader through the basic legal concepts which are of general application, including the different types of finance agreement that commonly exist. It will then move on to look at the three main areas of law which impact on this basic position and which complicate matters in practice:

- The statutory control of contract terms. This involves looking at the creation of implied terms, the circumstances in which the exclusion of those terms is possible, and how breaches of those terms are to be dealt with, together with some general consideration of when and why other contract terms will be considered 'unfair';

- The general regulation of Finance Companies, most of which are in practice authorised by the Financial Conduct Authority (FCA); and

- More targeted consumer protection controls on the behaviour of Finance Companies operating within the motor finance sector; in particular, those aspects of consumer protection control which have their roots in, and apply most often to agreements regulated by, the Consumer Credit Act 1974 (the 1974 Act).

However, in order to understand how this layered approach works, it is important to appreciate why it exists. Essentially, UK law has two fundamental intertwining strands: the general "common law" which is created and developed piecemeal by the Courts through a sequence of decisions by judges, and "statute law" which is created by Parliament and developed by both Courts and Regulators. If put in economic terms, the common law can be seen as being the product of market forces, with Customers, Finance Companies and Sellers all struggling for individual advantage, with statute law being created by Parliament and Regulators when it is felt that the results of those market forces are not acceptable for reasons of social policy.

It is also important to recognise that both types of law are constantly developing and moving on, as Courts and Regulators find new reasons to exercise control over the areas for which they are responsible. This point is important for two reasons. Firstly, because what is in force and/or acceptable today may well not be so tomorrow; and secondly, because it is essential to understand what a given form of regulation is trying to achieve, in order to work out how to properly comply with it.

Another way of looking at this second reason is through the phrase, 'For every rule, there is a scam'. In other words, underlying each and every regulation is a belief that market forces were in some way failing the reasonable interests of Customers, thereby making it necessary for Sellers and/or Finance Companies to be forced to either do, or not do, something in order to correct the position. This is, of course, the fundamental precept of all compliance law. Unfortunately, those working in the motor finance industry, including the lawyers, all too often fail to interpret compliance requirements in a purposive manner. The detail of those requirements is obviously important. However, too narrow a focus on detail can make it difficult to interpret the requirements themselves. In practice, this detail often becomes easier to apply if viewed in the context of the wider regulatory picture, with an understanding of the thinking that lies behind the seemingly inevitable march of increasing regulatory compliance.

That said, not all motor finance transactions involve all possible legal elements; as we will see, business transactions with corporate entities are, by and large, much more straightforward than retail transactions with consumers. As such, some readers may feel that large sections of this book do not apply to their work. However, a large part of understanding motor finance law as a whole involves getting to grips with these more complex areas, if only to be able to appreciate why and how they do not apply to corporate transactions.

In addition to the basic legal concepts and the way in which they are enforced by Courts and Regulators, we will also glance occasionally at some examples of the issues that commonly arise within motor finance law, and how they often work out in practice. Throughout this process, we will be avoiding much of the detail that inevitably complicates consideration of the legal issues underpinning any specific motor finance transaction. This is deliberate. The aim of this book is not to provide detailed answers to all the legal questions that may arise in connection with motor finance transactions. Rather, the intention is to provide readers with the equivalent of the picture which accompanies a complicated jigsaw puzzle; a general understanding that will equip them to both formulate the right questions and to search through the available detailed resources that exist in order to answer those questions.

CHAPTER TWO
THE APPROACH TO REGULATION

To begin with, some thoughts on the history of consumer credit regulation and the manner in which it has grown in application since the first Bills of Sale legislation in the mid 1800s. Those whose business consists entirely of agreements which are unregulated by the 1974 Act may be tempted to skip over this section. However, the concepts which apply to agreements regulated by the 1974 Act and the plethora of regulations which surround it (CCA Law) are a good example of the general approach adopted by Parliament and Regulators to a variety of compliance issues. Furthermore, even those who only engage in transactions outside CCA Law need to have a broad understanding of its application in order to be able to explain to Customers why the rights which the 1974 Act contains do not apply to the current circumstances.

Essentially, as already mentioned, for every rule there is a scam. Over time, we have as a society moved away from the *laissez-faire* approach to commercial affairs of the early Victorian governments, and successive Regulators have identified specific activities on the part of Finance Companies and Sellers which are felt to be inappropriate and require correction. For example, the long-standing requirement[1] for the prescribed information in a regulated agreement to *"...be of a colour which is readily distinguishable from..."* the background on which it is displayed is clearly the direct result of past unscrupulous Finance Companies using colour differentials to prevent Customers from easily reading such information.

That argument will not in itself be surprising to many, but it is the corollary which is so often overlooked by those who are unfamiliar with CCA Law, even experienced lawyers. This position can best be summed up in the question *"Where in CCA Law does it say I can do that?"*, to which the answer is often *"nowhere"*. The fact is that despite the extent

1 https://www.legislation.gov.uk/uksi/1983/1553/regulation/6/made

and breadth of its scope, CCA Law is not intended to be an all-encompassing bible containing the solution to all possible queries. As a result, large swathes of general law apply as much in the CCA regulated arena as they do to any other form of lending activity. In particular, the standard contractual position still applies to a CCA regulated agreement, and the principles which underpin the ownership of assets are unchanged.

What can be different is the detailed application of the general law. CCA Law, in common with much consumer protection, should be viewed not as a wholesale replacement for the general law, but as an additional element which in specific circumstances says that lenders must do this, or can't do that. Once stated, this position appears obvious; however, it is all too often overlooked in practice.

In addition, an appreciation of the general manner in which consumer protection laws tend to come about is crucial to a proper understanding of both the meaning and application of the relevant legislation. It is wrong to push the point too far. As any judge would confirm, it is the wording of a contract or a piece of legislation that matters; what it actually says, rather than what a party to the contract or even the legislator intended it to say. On the other hand, an unfortunate number of legal requirements in the regulated arena are less than clear. In addition, many are designed in an anti-avoidance manner which deliberately avoids black and white rules in favour of more nebulous concepts such as 'fairness'.

Detailed textual analysis of a provision can often produce alternative readings, and lawyers are paid to argue in favour of the interpretation which happens to coincide with their client's wishes. In such cases, or perhaps where simply trying to work out how to comply with a requirement on a day to day basis, it is important to look for the intention behind the provision and to interpret it in a purposive manner. Taking this approach cannot change the clear meaning of words; some provisions can only have one meaning, no matter how absurd the results. However, a reasonable understanding of what a provision is trying to achieve is often key to the practical application of its terms.

Unfortunately, the current approach to consumer credit regulation is fragmented and sometimes inconsistent. A high level understanding of why this is the case can assist practical application day to day.

For a start, there are broadly two different approaches to financial services compliance, which for present purposes we can loosely (if a little inaccurately) label the OFT and FCA approaches. These approaches were in theory combined in 2014 when the OFT was abolished and the FCA took over responsibility for consumer credit, but the result is perhaps best described as a bit of a 'cut and shut'. As such, an understanding of how each approach works helps avoid some of the pitfalls that have been created.

The OFT approach was centred on the highly complex and technical set of regulations which have over the years been constructed around the 1974 Act. The 1974 Act is effectively 'cradle to grave', being divided into twelve parts which dealt with:

I. The OFT and its functions

II. General concepts applying to regulated agreements

III. Licensing arrangements

IV. Seeking business

V. Entering into regulated agreements

VI. Matters arising during the life of agreements

VII. Dealing with default and termination

VIII. Taking security

IX. Oversight by the courts

X. Ancillary businesses, such as credit broking and debt collection

XI. Enforcement of the Act itself

XII. Miscellaneous items, including a list of definitions

The various ancillary regulations then provided detail in respect of a number of areas, including the core issues of:

- Exemptions
- How charges for credit must be disclosed
- Advertising requirements
- Pre-contract disclosure
- Form and content of agreements and security
- Provision of 'in-life' information
- Early settlement
- Default and similar notices

The application of this complex set of rules has always been fraught with peril for Finance Companies. The structure was always intended to cover a wide variety of circumstances, and has proved surprisingly able to adjust to a modern finance market which is radically different to that which existed in the 1970s. Nevertheless, there have always been provisions which raised problems of interpretation, such as the concept of multiple agreements set out in section 18. Furthermore, some of the upgrading that has taken place in the last 15 to 20 years has frankly not been as well drafted as the original 1974 Act, which has introduced unnecessary complications and issues for Finance Companies.

The greatest problem for Finance Companies, though, has always been the binary nature of the OFT approach to compliance; everything is black or white, and the consequences of any failure can be severe. The most egregious example of this must be the problems arising from the application of sections 77A (annual statements for fixed sum credit agreements) and 86B (notices of sums in arrears), of which more later. The intention behind the introduction of these provisions was admirable. However, the drafting of them was poor and has created much uncertainty, with the impact on a Finance Company of any error being in many cases out of all proportion to the breach.

This approach also created a fundamental problem for Customers, in that if a Finance Company were acting strictly within the letter of the law, potential or even actual Customer detriment was broadly irrelevant. In addition, because the structure which underpinned the approach was set out in legislation which could only be changed by Parliament, any changes to deal with new issues or market development involved a time consuming and costly process. In the final few years of its existence, the OFT made great efforts to broaden its approach to compliance, partly by extending the scope of the licensing regime to cover issues such as competence, and partly by issuing extended guidance designed to promote acceptable Finance Company behaviour. Even these efforts, though, were hampered by the nature of the regime, and by the OFT's simple lack of funds to enforce its writ.

The FCA approach to compliance does not by any means abandon the use of detailed rules. Indeed the FCA Handbook of Rules and Guidance contains much that is as obscure and difficult to apply as anything the OFT approach was ever able to create. However, the fundamental nature of the approach is very different. Essentially, the FCA takes the view that following strict rules for, say, the form and content of documentation is a secondary compliance activity; the primary compliance activity of any authorised firm is to run its business in a manner that is both competent and fair to its Customers. If that happens, good results for those Customers will be inevitable.

A full analysis of the FCA approach is outside the scope of this book. Essentially, though, it is underpinned by a regulatory structure that begins with 11 Principles for Business. These principles are broad in definition, and in some cases amount to no more than a statement of good corporate governance, but it is worth highlighting the following[2]:

- Principle 1 – *"A firm must conduct its business with integrity"*
- Principle 2 – *"A firm must conduct its business with due skill, care and diligence"*
- Principle 3 – *"A firm must take reasonable care to organise and control its affairs responsibly and effectively, with adequate risk management systems"*
- Principle 6 – *"A firm must pay due regard to the interests of its customers and treat them fairly"*
- Principle 11 – *"A firm must deal with its regulators in an open and cooperative way, and must disclose to the FCA appropriately anything relating to the firm of which that regulator would reasonably expect notice"*

The Principles are reinforced by large numbers of Rules, some of which apply to all firms, but others only to those who are engaged in a particular undertaking. These are in turn supported by Guidance, which outlines the FCA's thinking on the application of a Rule in a given context. However, many of these requirements are deliberately couched in broad terms to allow them to be applicable to a variety of circumstances, with each firm obliged to interpret the requirements in accordance with its own individual circumstances, and to apply them in a manner that is consistent with the Principles.

This results in a structure that is inherently flexible. Although it is constrained by framework legislation, in particular the Financial Services and Markets Act 2000 (FSMA) and the Financial Services and Markets Act 2000 (Regulated Activities) Order 2001 (the RAO), the Handbook not only has the force of law, but can be amended by the FCA itself

2 https://www.handbook.fca.org.uk/handbook/PRIN/2/1.html

within a reasonably short period under its rule making powers. Furthermore, the FCA is not in the game of enforcing "black and white" rules. Both the Rules and the Guidance need to be interpreted in accordance with the Principles. More fundamentally, the exercise by the FCA of its investigatory and enforcement powers is not confined to breaches of the Rules and Guidance, but extends to any activity which the FCA considers to be in breach of the Principles.

In the circumstances, any application of the Handbook needs to consider the Principles at every stage; in particular Principle 6, which is usually referred to as "Treating Customers Fairly" or just "TCF". The result is a compliance landscape which may be black and white at the extremities, but is mostly composed of shades of grey, with more than one "acceptable" answer to many questions. This means that the FCA approach is much more closely aligned to other forms of mainstream compliance regulation, such as data protection, anti-money laundering and consumer contract protection, than the OFT approach could ever have been.

This FCA approach is also the reason that most Finance Companies still need to be mindful of much of the Handbook, even when operating outside the scope of CCA Law. The FCA regulates an authorised Finance Company as a whole, not just one section of its activity. Many of its Rules are intended to be of general application, and even those which are not can still be relevant if it can be reasonably argued that compliance is a matter of TCF, a principle that of course applies to all the Finance Companies customers, not just those who enter into agreements regulates by the 1974 Act. An authorised Finance Company can interpret TCF differently as between its business and consumer Customers, but it still needs to apply the principle to them all.

In practice, whenever a compliance breach occurs the two crucial questions which the FCA will require to be answered are:

- did the Finance Company take reasonable steps in line with the Handbook requirements to try to avoid the breach; and

- has there been any Customer detriment?

The FCA usual position is that a Finance Company that has genuinely attempted to apply the Rules and Guidance in line with the Principles may need to amend its practices in the light of a breach, and will certainly need to compensate its Customers for any detriment caused, but should have little to fear in terms of sanctions. On the other hand, a Finance Company that has made no real attempt to apply the Handbook properly will almost certainly face sanctions, regardless of whether there has in fact been any detriment caused its Customers, or even a breach at all.

The flexibility of the FCA approach may appear at first sight to create uncertainty, and many Finance Companies familiar with the OFT approach were concerned by the 2014 transfer of CCA responsibility. However, the benefits of the approach are considerable, not least the focus on Customer detriment as the basis for any remediation. By way of example, section 86B has no application to peer-to peer lending activity, simply because such activity was relatively unknown when the section was introduced and it was just not drafted so as to apply. This was later felt to be an omission, but amending the 1974 Act would have been a major exercise, so nothing could be done until the FCA took over CCA regulation. At that stage, the FCA incorporated into the new Consumer Credit Sourcebook section of the Handbook (CONC) similar requirements to those set out in section 86B, but with one important exception; no automatic sanctions for non-compliance. As a result, failure to comply with this CONC requirement will only result in a remediation payment being made to an affected Customer if and to the extent that any detriment has in fact been caused.

This example, however, also highlights the unfortunate nature of the current CCA regime. The OFT itself may be no more, but its approach lives on in that much of the pre-existing legislation was preserved at the time of transfer. This was a practical necessity, but it does mean that the current CCA regime encompasses two distinct and not always compatible approaches to compliance. The FCA is considering the position, and is required to decide by 2019 how much more of the old regime it wishes to take under its direct control via FSMA. Unless and until this happens, though, this dual approach remains, and early indications are that the FCA is not anxious to struggle with the inevitable issues which such a transfer would involve.

CHAPTER THREE
BASIC CONCEPTS

Ownership, possession and use

'Ownership' of an asset is a complex subject in itself, but for present purposes the important thing to remember is that it is not a single indivisible right; rather, ownership is a bundle of rights which can be split between different parties. In the context of motor vehicle finance, the three core rights/questions are:

- Title – who has the right to sell the vehicle;
- Possession – who has the right to hold on to the vehicle; and
- Use – who has the right to drive the vehicle around?

Usually, outside finance arrangements, the owner of a vehicle will be entitled to exercise all of these rights; they will be able to sell the vehicle if they wish to do so, but in the meantime are entitled to keep it in their possession and to make such use of it as they wish. Finance arrangements, however, often involve these rights being split between different parties. For example, a Finance Company will normally retain title to the vehicle whilst contractually passing the rights of possession and use over to the Customer under the terms of the finance agreement. This agreement may or may not involve a later transfer of title to the Customer, but either way it will need to contain provisions designed to protect the Finance Company's interest in the vehicle by placing obligations and limitations on the Customer regarding the use and possession of it.

Furthermore, though not directly related to finance arrangements, it is worth highlighting that there are more general circumstances in which these rights of ownership can be split between parties. In particular, for present purposes:

- Charges – charges are a contractual arrangement under which the owner of a vehicle transfers certain rights of ownership to a third party, usually by way of security. In such circumstances, use and possession of the vehicle will remain with the owner. However, the owner's right of title will be restricted, in that the charge will prevent them from selling without the permission of the other party. Furthermore, that other party will usually be given the right to sell the vehicle and pass good title to a third party in specified circumstances, and the charge agreement will again contain obligations and limitations in respect of the owner's use and possession, in order to maintain the value of the vehicle in case it ever becomes necessary for the power of sale to be exercised;

- Liens – often wrongly thought of as being a form of charge, liens are in fact all about possession. It is possible for a contractual lien to create a power of sale, but such liens are unusual in practice. The vast majority of liens are no more than a right to hold onto a vehicle until certain conditions have been satisfied, most usually the payment of money. By far the most commonplace example of the exercise of a lien in respect of motor vehicles is the right of a vehicle repairer to hold onto the vehicle until a repair bill has been paid. This is a 'common law' right which can be exercised by any repairer of goods against the owner, even if that owner is a Finance Company and the arrangements for repair were actually entered into by the Customer. However, it is essential to remember that a common law lien is only a right to possession. It gives the repairer no rights of use or sale; neither does it allow for ancillary charges, such as in respect of storage;

- Statutory bodies – the detail is beyond the scope of this book, but it is worth noting in passing that there are circumstances in which some statutory bodies can become entitled to hold and/or dispose of a vehicle against the wishes of the true owner, regardless of whether that owner is a Finance Company or a Customer.

What is a CCA 'regulated' agreement?

Almost the first point of confusion in the area of consumer credit law is that it doesn't just cover credit; nor does it only apply to 'consumers' in the usual sense of the word. As we will see, contracts for the hire of goods can be regulated, as are certain types of business contract. In addition, there are many 'consumer' credit and hire agreements that are not regulated by the CCA. The identification of a CCA regulated agreement is a two-stage process, and we will look at credit and hire contracts in turn.

Section 8(1) defines[1] a consumer credit agreement as "*...an agreement between an individual ("the debtor") and any other person ("the creditor") by which the creditor provides the debtor with credit of any amount.*"

The first point to note about this definition is just how wide it is in application. It is deliberately designed to encompass all contractual arrangements under which an individual is provided with credit. However, it is also necessary to appreciate that courtesy of section 189, the 1974 Act has its own special definition of an "individual" which includes:

- a partnership consisting of two or three persons not all of whom are bodies corporate; and
- an unincorporated body of persons which does not consist entirely of bodies corporate and is not a partnership.

As a result, the definition of a consumer credit agreement (whether or not regulated) not only encompasses any contractual grant of credit made to an individual in the normal sense of the word, whether acting

1 https://www.legislation.gov.uk/ukpga/1974/39/section/8

in a personal or business capacity, but also to one made to small partnerships and unincorporated associations (for example members clubs). In practice, it applies to nearly all credit arrangements except those made with corporate entities such as limited liability companies and partnerships, and partnerships of 4 or more partners.

To help avoid confusion, it should be noted that for FSMA purposes the RAO adopts a slightly different approach. Use of the word 'individual' by the RAO and by the FCA in its Handbook is restricted to the everyday meaning of the word. Accordingly, the RAO and the Handbook refer to an individual or 'relevant recipient of credit'; the latter being defined to cover the gap between the normal meaning of 'individual' and the extended section 189 definition. This rather clunky approach becomes doubly confusing when applied (as it is) to those who enter into consumer hire agreements, which contain no element of credit!

Of course, this all begs the question of what is 'credit'. Again, for anti-avoidance purposes, this concept is deliberately defined in as wide a manner as possible; section 9(1) says[2] that it includes "...*a cash loan, and any other form of financial accommodation*". Entire books have been written about this one subject. For present purposes it is enough to note that all the commonplace forms of deferred payment for the purchase of motor vehicles, such as hire purchase, conditional sale and credit sale, are within the definition of 'credit'.

On the other hand, although hire purchase is a form of 'credit' (because section 9(3) says so), an ordinary hire contract is not; it has a separate identity in the form of a 'consumer hire agreement', defined by section 15(1) as[3]:

> "... *an agreement made by a person with an individual (the "hirer") for the bailment or (in Scotland) the hiring of goods to the hirer, being an agreement which—*

2 https://www.legislation.gov.uk/ukpga/1974/39/section/9

3 https://www.legislation.gov.uk/ukpga/1974/39/section/15

(a) is not a hire-purchase agreement, and

(b) is capable of subsisting for more than three months."

The second of these criteria is the reason why short-term vehicle rental contracts, such as the hire of a car or van for a few days, always contain a standard clause restricting the maximum possible period of hire; usually to thirty days, but at the very most to ninety days. This is to ensure that the agreement remains outside the scope of the 1974 Act.

As with credit, section 15(1) does not discriminate between hirers acting in a personal or business capacity, and of course the section 189 definition of an 'individual' extends it to hire agreements with small partnerships and unincorporated associations, as does the FSMA/RAO use of the phrase 'relevant recipient of credit'.

To avoid similar confusion to that which the FCA has created by use of this phrase, the draftsman of the 1974 Act drew a distinction between the parties to a credit agreement (the 'creditor' and the 'debtor') and those to a hire agreement (the 'owner' and the 'hirer'). This distinction is particularly helpful when it comes to distinguishing between those sections of the 1974 Act that apply to both forms of agreement, and those which only apply to either credit or hire

Having deliberately drawn the boundaries for consumer credit and consumer hire agreements as widely as possible, the 1974 Act then takes us on to the second and crucial stage in identifying a 'regulated' agreement. Essentially, all consumer credit and hire agreements are to be treated as regulated unless they fall within one of a number of specific and tightly defined exemptions. Prior to 2014, these exemptions were part of the 1974 Act itself, but are now to be found within the definitions set out in the RAO.

The exemptions applying to credit agreements are set out in Articles 60C to 60H of the RAO, and those applying to hire agreements in Articles 60O to 60Q. Many of these exemptions are highly technical, and for the purposes of this book consideration is limited to the two which most commonly apply, usually referred to as the 'business' and 'high net worth' exemptions.

The business exemption is based on the value of the transaction. The 1974 Act originally applied only to agreements which had a value below a specified level, but this was abolished by the Consumer Credit Act 2006 (the 2006 Act). The limit had been adjusted on a number of occasions, but immediately prior to its abolition, the 1974 Act did not apply where the amount of credit to be provided, or the aggregate rentals to be paid under a hire agreement (including VAT), exceeded £25,000. Since the limit was abolished, there has been no general restriction on the application of the 1974 Act by value. However, there was much debate at the time about whether the 1974 Act should continue to apply to business transactions. In the end, a compromise solution emerged; business arrangements involving sole traders, small partnerships and unincorporated associations would continue to be regulated, but only where they fell within the existing £25,000 limit.

As a result, any agreement providing for credit or total rentals exceeding that figure will be exempt from CCA regulation if it is entered into 'wholly or predominantly' for the purposes of a business carried on by the Customer. Whether that is the case is a pure question of fact; this is not, as is sometimes mistakenly believed, an optional exemption. However, to limit uncertainty for Finance Companies, the RAO does provide that if the agreement contains a declaration by the Customer in the prescribed form, then it will be presumed to be exempt as long as the Finance Company did not know, or have reason to suspect, that the agreement was not actually for business purposes.

The 'high net worth' exemption, by contrast, only applies at the option of the Customer. The exemption is based on the assumption that an individual of "high net worth" will be sufficiently sophisticated in financial terms as to be able to divest themselves of the protections of the 1974 Act, if they so wish. Whether or not this assumption is correct remains open to question, but the exemption is available if the relevant criteria are satisfied.

There is, however, a value limitation applicable to credit agreement (though not to hire agreements). The exemption is incompatible with the EU Consumer Credit Directive (the CCD); accordingly, it is only available if the amount of credit to be provided exceeds the CCD value limit of £60,260.

In either case, there are also strict criteria for the identification of a 'high net worth' Customer. Essentially, during the previous financial year they must have either had an income (net of tax) exceeding £150,000, or assets (excluding their residence and pension arrangements) exceeding £500,000.

In addition, the agreement needs to contain a declaration by the Customer which:

- confirms that they have received a statement in the required format identifying them as an HNW individual (usually provided by an appropriately qualified accountant): and
- acknowledges that they are knowingly giving up their CCA rights.

Onc final point regarding the categorisation of credit and hire agreements. It is often suggested that they fall into two categories; regulated and unregulated. However, this categorisation can be unhelpful, because there are some elements of CCA regulation which apply to, or in respect of, agreements which are otherwise 'exempt'. In particular, exempt credit agreements are still subject to the unfair relationship provisions of section 140A. In addition, the regulation by the 1974 Act of ancillary finance activities such as credit broking, debt collecting, debt counselling and debt adjusting extends to engaging in such activities in respect of any consumer credit or consumer hire agreement, regardless of whether it is regulated. The somewhat counter-intuitive result of this is that whilst (for example) the Finance Company entering into an exempt credit agreement does not need to be authorised by the FCA to do so, a credit broking Seller that makes the introduction does.

Creditworthiness, Forbearance and Vulnerability

In addition to the specific provisions laid down in the 1974 Act itself, Finance Companies have for some years also been subject to the wider set of rules and guidance contained in the FCA's Handbook; in particular CONC. In many ways, the Handbook provisions are not dissimilar to the concept of section 140A, being greatly based on the FCA principle of 'Treating Customers Fairly', and TCF most obviously manifests itself in the shape of the concepts of 'creditworthiness', 'forbearance' and 'vulnerability'. The last two of these concepts are particularly applicable in the context of collections and recoveries.

Generally speaking, Finance Companies who want to stay in business for any length of time do not lend money to a Customer unless they think it is likely to be repaid. However, the CCD introduced a specific requirement for them to consider the issue of 'creditworthiness' before entering into any agreement with a consumer. There is always an element of risk involved in providing credit, and Finance Companies engage in substantial amounts of analysis in order to keep that 'credit risk' within acceptable commercial limits. However, whilst credit risk is the essential element of any lending decision from the Finance Company's point of view, it is not the whole story by any means. The requirements in this regard have recently been clarified by the FCA, but the general position is unchanged; in addition to considering the risk to themselves arising from a failure by a Customer to repay the credit (on time or at all), Finance Companies are required to further consider the risk to the Customer arising from such a failure (referred to as 'affordability risk').

Affordability is a difficult concept to pin down in practice, not least because it involves both objective and subjective factors. However, whilst the details of an affordability assessment can be difficult to develop, the principle is fairly easy to state; based on all the relevant evidence, does it appear likely that the Customer will be in a position to make the anticipated payments under the agreement in a 'sustainable manner'. To put it another way, the Finance Company is required to look at the potential for the commitments under the agreement to adversely impact the Customer's financial situation, both now and in the future.

An example from the world of pay day lending may assist understanding of the difference between credit risk and affordability risk. It was common practice for pay day lenders to require a loan to be repaid when the Customer had funds available in their bank account; usually on the date of salary payment. As such, the credit risk to the pay day lender could be relatively low. On the other hand, once the loan and charges had been repaid, the Customer would still need to cover their everyday financial commitments for the rest of that month, and would often struggle to do so. As such, the affordability risk to the Customer could be relatively high.

As regards forbearance, the Handbook states[4] that: '*A firm must treat Customers in default or in arrears difficulties with forbearance and due consideration.*' In particular, the firm must allow the Customer reasonable time and opportunity to remedy any default or arrears; it must also take steps to refer the Customer to sources of free and impartial debt advice.

In one sense, forbearance is an extension of the concept of affordability discussed elsewhere, in that a firm should not be putting pressure on a Customer to enter into any repayment plan which is going to adversely impact their general financial circumstances. As a result, a Finance Company has to ensure that any action it takes in respect of recovery and collections is proportionate. This, as always, involves a balancing exercise between the interests of the Finance Company and those of the Customer, with the Finance Company being required to demonstrate that it has paid due attention to those of the Customer.

In addition, a Finance Company will need to ensure that it has policies and procedures in place in order to deal with Customers which it knows, or reasonably suspects, to be 'vulnerable'. This is not a precise concept, and is in many ways an extension of the general principles of

4 https://www.handbook.fca.org.uk/handbook/CONC/7/3.html

TCF. Applying TCF is a fluid exercise. What may be fair in respect of one Customer may not be fair in respect of another; indeed, what may be fair in respect of a given Customer at a given time, may not be fair at another time. This balancing exercise is constant, and any circumstances which tend to make a Customer more vulnerable than they might otherwise be, need to be taken into account.

At the more extreme end of the spectrum, Customers with mental health issues must be seen as particularly vulnerable. However, since vulnerability is a spectrum, Finance Companies need to ensure that any activity regarding a Customer (including, but by no means limited to collections and recoveries activity) is geared to the potentially shifting vulnerability of a Customer. A Customer in financial difficulties, or suffering from health problems, loss of job or marital difficulties, is thereby likely to be more vulnerable, and all such factors need to be taken into account as part of the balancing exercise.

Lastly, it is worth bearing in mind that whilst the Handbook Rules in question may only directly apply to certain Customers, the concepts of creditworthiness, forbearance and vulnerability are good examples of issues that must be treated by authorised firms as being of wider application, given that the principles which underpin them, particularly TCF, are of general application. That is not to say that the same approach needs to be taken in every case; the approach can (and indeed should) be tailored to the relevant context. Nevertheless, it must be possible in every case to say that the approach taken is consistent with the underlying principles. For example, the Rules on creditworthiness do not apply directly to hire agreements. However, it is difficult to see how a Finance Company might be able to justify not adopting a similar approach to a Customer's affordability risk arising from a given level of payments, simply because the proposed agreement is one of hire rather than credit.

Total Charge for Credit/APR

These two linked concepts are fundamental to the operation of the 1974 Act. It is clearly important that consumers are informed about the true cost of the credit they are minded to take out, in a form that allows them to compare alternative means of obtaining that credit. The regulations controlling the identification of the total charge for credit are particularly obscure. However, in terms of motor vehicle finance, the basic concept is straightforward; anything that is payable in connection with the credit which isn't part of the 'cash price' of the vehicle, is a charge.

It must always be remembered that an Annual Percentage Rate (APR) is not an interest rate. Interest will often be the primary charge to be included within the APR calculation, but the APR and the Interest Rate for an agreement will only be the same if the interest rate in question is an 'effective annual rate', and there are no other charges payable. Use of 'flat' interest rates, which do not allow for any element of compounding, can be misleading to consumers. Likewise, the use of fixed charges to reduce the element of interest charged can make it hard for consumers to compare different products, and hide the fact that an agreement with a lower rate of interest is actually more expensive overall.

An APR is an annualised expression in percentage terms of all charges falling due under the agreement. Once the total charges have been identified, the Finance Company is required to apply a complicated actuarial formula in order to calculate the APR by reference to the actual timing of the credits, charges and repayments that should occur throughout the term of the agreement. APRs have their drawbacks, and can be misleading for both short and long term finance arrangements. Nevertheless, for most vehicle finance agreements they serve their intended use by being a useful way of comparing the cost of different types of arrangement.

Unenforceability

Unenforceability under the 1974 Act is a difficult concept, and there has been considerable legal dispute over the years as to what it means. The situation is further complicated because unenforceability broadly falls into two types:

- In some cases, the agreement will be unenforceable until the designated authority (usually the Court, but in some cases the FCA) has given permission for enforcement to take place; but

- In other cases, the agreement can only become enforceable again if the Finance Company remedies the breach, which can sometimes be difficult or even impossible.

Application of the concept of unenforceability is further complicated by the range of interpretations that can be placed on the meaning of the word. There are those who argue that any action which a Finance Company takes in order to try to make a Customer pay when the Customer is unwilling or unable to do so, amounts to 'enforcement' for these purposes. This is, however, a very restricted view, and at the other end of the spectrum are those who argue that 'enforcement' should be given a strict legal meaning, thereby effectively limiting the concept to the enforcement of a court order.

Adopting a purposive approach to interpretation of the concept would suggest that neither of these extreme approaches can be right. The most restrictive interpretation would, by definition, prevent a Finance Company from carrying out certain actions, including the service of a Default Notice, which are prescribed by the 1974 Act as pre-requisites for the making of an application to the court for an enforcement order. On the other hand, there are many references within the 1974 Act which are clearly inconsistent with the 'court order' approach, not least the fact that retaking possession of the vehicle is specifically stated to be 'enforcement'.

As with so many such arguments, the answer must lie somewhere in between, and is probably context specific. In the absence of a clear indication from the courts as to interpretation of 1974 Act unenforceability, it must be assumed that a Finance Company is entitled to take steps to require a Customer to comply with an unenforceable agreement, such as the sending of letters stating that it will arrange to terminate the agreement and repossess the vehicle if the Customer does not pay, provided that:

- the Finance Company does genuinely intend to take the indicated steps if the Customer does not comply; and
- the Finance Company clearly brings the fact of unenforceability to the attention of the Customer, so that they can make an informed decision as to whether to comply.

On this basis, a Finance Company is entitled to go through the process of default and termination, with a view to issuing court proceedings and obtaining an enforcement order if needs be. This approach is entirely in line with the 1974 Act itself, which provides in section 173 that whilst an attempt to contract out of its requirements is invalid, anything which may only be done 'on an order of the court or the FCA' may in fact also be done with the contemporaneous consent of the Customer. As FCA guidance indicates, any Customer consent must be genuine and informed; hence the need for the Finance Company to ensure that the Customer is informed of the fact and consequences of unenforceability.

As regards obtaining an enforcement order, this requires the Finance Company to make an application under Section 127 of the 1974 Act. This can, of course, only be done where the particular breach means that the agreement is unenforceable without an order of the court. As noted above, some breaches of the 1974 Act can only be remedied by the Finance Company itself, and if the Finance Company is for some reason unable to comply, then the breach can never be remedied and the agreement can never be enforced.

Updating the 1974 Act/the Consumer Credit Directive (CCD)

Even a cursory examination of the updating of the 1974 Act and its underlying regulations which has taken place over the past few years will reveal just how fragmented the whole area has become, as each new development is shoe horned uncomfortably into the existing structure. The 1974 Act, and the original regulations introduced (mostly) in 1983, created what was, with a few notable exceptions, a well drafted and coherent body of rules and requirements. Unfortunately, many of the changes introduced over the last fifteen or so years have added considerably to the complexity of the structure, and unfortunately many of them have not been well drafted so as to fit in seamlessly into the whole. In particular, the changes introduced in 2011 to bring the UK in line with the requirements of the CCD have fragmented the structure, so that different types of motor finance credit agreement now get dealt with in very different ways, depending on a number of factors.

This problem is most evident as regards the documentation and execution of regulated agreements. However, before looking at the detail, it is helpful to have a broad idea of the ground covered by the CCD changes, and which forms of regulated agreement fall inside and outside the relevant requirements. Unfortunately, getting an understanding of these issues is not helped by the fact that the CCD boundaries are not applied consistently. In advance, the Treasury's stated approach was that it would make only the minimum changes required to the existing CCA provisions in order to ensure CCD compliance. However, when it came to the detail, the Treasury could not resist extending some of these changes into areas that were strictly outside CCD scope.

As regards that scope, broadly the CCD does not apply to agreements:

- for hire;
- secured on land;
- for credit exceeding £60,260; or
- for business purposes.

As explained elsewhere, hire agreements do not involve credit, and secured lending was already the subject of other EU discussions; furthermore, outside the UK, the distinction between retail and business purpose agreements is better drawn. As such, three of these exemptions from the CCD are easily understood. The financial exemption seems rather arbitrary at first sight, but does have a reasonable explanation. For about 30 years, the 1974 Act incorporated a financial limit. UK consumer protection thinking had moved away from this approach by the time the CCD came to be, but the EU still took the view that such a limit should apply, and set the bar at 75,000 Euros. In accordance with a standard EU approach, the potential currency exchange fluctuation issue this might cause because the UK was outside the Eurozone was avoided by fixing the limit at the sterling equivalent on the date the CCD took effect; hence the figure of £60,260.

Applying the CCD was a relatively simple process for those EU countries which did not have complex existing consumer finance laws already in place. Many were able to adopt the CCD wholesale, as a standalone set of measures. The problem for the Uk was how incorporate the CCD regime within the pre-existing structure of the CCA, bearing in mind that;

- the 1974 Act has no financial limit and does extend to cover some, though not all, business purpose agreements;
- the CCD is what is known in EU law as a 'maximum harmonisation' directive, which requires the law in all member states to be identical; and
- the government was reluctant to abandon any part of the existing regime.

That existing regime was considerably more developed, and arguably much better, than was the norm in most other EU states. Unfortunately, the government approach inevitably led to the creation of a regime made up of multiple alternative requirements based on variations in context.

Understanding the practical application of this new regime was then further complicated by an additional issue; namely, the ability of Finance Companies in some circumstances to voluntarily adopt the CCD documentation requirements should they wish to do so. This was an entirely economic point. At the time the CCD changes were being discussed, many Finance Companies pointed out that it would make life prohibitively expensive for them (and therefore indirectly for Customers) if they were required to maintain distinct approaches for the documentation and execution of credit agreements that were inside and outside CCD scope. Accordingly, to avoid unnecessary system duplication, provisions were introduced to allow Finance Companies to opt-in to the relevant CCD requirements instead of those which would otherwise apply.

However, this ability to opt-in has its limits. It applies to unsecured credit-based arrangements, thereby allowing Finance Companies to adopt the CCD approach to documentation and execution in respect of credit agreements which are strictly outside CCD scope because they are above the £60,260 limit or are for business purposes. On the other hand, it has no application to hire agreements.

As a final general point, whenever looking at the detail of these alternative regimes, it is always worth remembering that the CCD is trying to address the same issues (real or perceived) that underpin the 1974 Act approach to the documentation and execution of regulated CCA agreements. It has always been a fundamental principle of CCA regulation that Customers need to be given the right information by Finance Companies in advance, so that they can make an informed decision as to whether they should enter into the finance agreement. Accordingly, leaving aside the technicalities of the regulations, both the CCD and 1974 Act versions of the regulations are trying to do much the same thing.

In fact, the CCD approach is in many ways to be preferred, for much the same reasons as the FCA approach to regulation has advantages over the OFT approach. Both the CCD and 1974 Act approaches require similar information to be given to Customers, in broadly similar ways. However, the 1974 Act approach is much more prescriptive about exactly how this is to be done, and in many ways produces documentation that is harder for Customers to understand. The CCD version is much more flexible, and actually allows Finance Companies to provide the relevant information in a manner that is often much easier for Customers to read and appreciate.

CHAPTER FOUR
TYPES OF VEHICLE FINANCE PRODUCT

Essentially, all vehicle finance comes down to the same thing. There is a Customer who wishes to obtain the use and/or ownership of a vehicle, but is not for some reason wanting to make an immediate purchase using existing funds. Instead, they need a Finance Company to assist in some way.

Broadly, whilst not hard and fast, it is helpful to group types of vehicle finance product into four broad categories:

- Loan
- Sale
- Hire
- Hire-purchase

Loan

A loan is the simplest form of vehicle finance product. At its most basic, the Finance Company simply agrees to advance a sum of money to the Customer so that the Customer can purchase the vehicle outright from the Seller. This will, of course, involve a contract of sale direct between the Seller and the Customer, and as we shall see, there are regulations which will impact on the terms of that contract. However, as far as the finance element of the transaction is concerned, the Customer simply agrees to repay the borrowed money to the Finance Company, along with any agreed charges.

As such, the terms of a basic loan agreement are quite simple. The contract will set out the amount and timing of the repayments which need to be made to the Finance Company, along with the consequences of any failure to repay in accordance with those terms; usually the payment of default interest, and the right of Finance Company to accelerate payment of the full balance due. There will be little or no attempt by the Finance Company to control the use or possession of the vehicle by the Customer.

Sale

As an alternative to the outright cash sale of a motor vehicle by a Seller to a Customer (whether or not funded by a loan), there are two commonplace forms of finance product which are intended to spread the cost of the exercise. In both cases, there will be a single contract under which the Customer agrees to purchase the vehicle, and to pay for it by instalments over a specified period of time. Essentially, this contract will combine the usual terms applicable to a sale with additional terms similar to those of a loan; setting out the payments that need to be made and the consequences of a failure by the Customer to comply.

Where the two types of contract vary is over the point at which ownership of the vehicle will pass to the Customer. In one form, known as Credit Sale, the Customer becomes the owner of the vehicle up front. Accordingly, as with a loan, there is little or no attempt by the Finance Company to control exactly what the Customer does with the vehicle during the repayment period. The position is very different for the other form of sale finance product, which is known as Conditional Sale. In this case there is an essential condition attached to the sale agreement; namely, that the Customer will only become the owner of the vehicle if and when the repayments are completed. This provision for 'retention of title' in the vehicle has substantial consequences for the content of the sale contract. In addition to clauses dealing with payments and the acceleration of the balance in the event of breach, the provider of the finance (which may be either a Finance Company or a Seller) has to consider the possibility that the vehicle will need to be recovered and sold so that the proceeds can be used to discharge at least part of that balance. Accordingly, a Conditional Sale Agreement needs to contain clauses which are intended to safeguard the sale value of the vehicle whilst it is in The Customer's possession. These clauses will allow for normal, everyday use by the Customer, usually referred to as 'fair wear and tear', but will otherwise control the possession and use of the vehicle by the Customer. The agreement will also set out the circumstances in which the Customer's rights in respect of the vehicle can be terminated, so that it can be repossessed and sold, and provide for payment of any shortfall by the Customer.

As indicated above, the owner of the vehicle who enters into a Conditional Sale Agreement may either be a Seller or a Finance Company. In practice, of course, most Sellers are not in the business of providing motor vehicle finance, so the vast majority of Credit and Conditional Sale Agreements are entered into by Finance Companies. It is, though, important to appreciate that when a Finance Company does so, it enters into two sale contracts; one for the supply of the vehicle to the Customer, but also an initial contract to purchase the vehicle from the Seller. In many circumstances this will be academic, but it becomes highly relevant if the Customer encounters problems with the vehicle. If that happens, the Finance Company is directly liable for those problems and will not be entitled to be paid (either in full, or perhaps even at all) unless it is contractually able to require the Seller to deal with them. The Customer and the Seller will almost certainly deal with the problems direct, and ultimately the Seller should always be responsible for making things right, but both the Customer and the Finance Company need to remain aware of the true contractual position in order to ensure they can achieve a satisfactory solution to the problems

Hire

A hire agreement involves no transfer of title; it is a contractual arrangement under which a Finance Company as the owner of a vehicle passes over use and possession to the Customer, in return for which the Customer agrees to pay rent for the vehicle during the period of hire. Indeed, it is an essential element of a hire agreement that there is no right for the Customer to take ownership, and any mutual expectation that title will (or even may) pass would affect the ability of the Finance Company to treat the agreement as one of hire for tax purposes. Since the Finance Company relies on this tax treatment to underpin the finance arrangements, hire agreements will always provide for the vehicle to be returned for sale by the Finance Company.

Strictly, a hire agreement is a contract for services. This creates a distinction between hire and sale agreements in respect of their VAT treatment. Generally, an agreement for the sale of a vehicle creates a VAT liability as at the date of sale, which the Finance Company has to pass over to HMRC. In contrast, VAT is payable under a hire agreement in respect of each rental, as and when it falls due. From the point of view of a retail Customer, this distinction is academic; however, it can be important in respect of business transactions, because of the way in which VAT payments and claims need to be made.

In practice, there are a number of different types of hire agreement available in the vehicle finance market, and it is important to realise that the differences between them are much less in legal terms than might immediately appear. In particular, there is simply no legal difference between a 'lease' agreement and a 'hire' agreement. Lease and hire are just different ways of saying the same thing.

In practice, the only major difference between types of hire agreement is the distinction between 'finance' and 'operating' leases, which is actually a product of the different accounting practice that applies to each.

Under the terms of a finance lease, the full initial cost of the vehicle, together with the Finance Company's charges, is repaid by the Customer through the rentals. These arrangements are accordingly often referred to as 'full pay out', and the Finance Company really has little or no real interest in the value of the vehicle once it has been paid for in full. For this reason, a finance lease will contain provision for the residual value of the vehicle at the end of the hire term to be transferred to the Customer, usually in the form of a rebate of rentals paid once the vehicle has been returned and sold by the Finance Company. In other words, the Customer cannot become the owner of the vehicle, but still receives the lion's share of the resale value in the same way as an owner would; the Finance Company's interest is limited to an administrative charge, usually in the region of 5 to 10% of the resale price.

Under the terms of an operating lease the Finance Company does not recover its full initial outlay during the hire period. Instead, the rentals payable by the Customer cover only the anticipated depreciation in the value of the vehicle during that period, together with the Finance Company's charges. At the end of the hire period, the vehicle will be still be returned and sold, but the Finance Company will retain all of the proceeds as part of the repayment of its initial outlay.

Generally, for a hire agreement to qualify as an operating lease, the Finance Company needs to be receiving more than 10% of its recovery by way of the net proceeds of sale. The anticipated sale proceeds built into the rental calculation are usually referred to as the 'residual value' of the vehicle, or R.V. As long as the vehicle meets the return conditions set out in the hire agreement, the Finance Company cannot recover any shortfall from the Customer if the net proceeds of sale turn out to be less than the RV, but it will be entitled to keep any surplus on sale.

In one sense, the purest form of operating lease is the short-term or 'spot hire' agreement operated by vehicle rental companies. These agreements are typically only for a few days or months, with the rentals paid representing only a fraction of the original value of the vehicle. In this case, the vehicle rental company will enter into multiple hire agreements with different Customers before selling the vehicle. By contrast, longer term vehicle operating leases will typically be an agreement with a single Customer lasting for a period of years, at the end of which the vehicle will be sold. Both are, though, just different forms of operating lease.

As already mentioned, the reasons behind the existence of finance and operating leases are the different accounting and tax treatments accorded to each, which affect both the Finance Company and a business Customer. In many ways this is all academic for retail Customers, who will not be putting the rentals through their business accounts, nor making VAT reclaims. However, they are still able to benefit from the different rental structures which the Finance Company can put in place.

The reality is more complex, but in simple terms a finance lease will have higher interim rentals because the Customer is repaying all of the Finance Company's outlay, but the Customer gets the value of the vehicle at the end of the hire period. Under an operating lease, the rentals would tend to be lower because only a part of the initial outlay is being repaid (though this reduction is to some extent offset by the higher charges which will accrue because a substantial part of that outlay is being deferred until the end of the hire period); however, the Customer has no interest in the value of the vehicle at the end.

Compared to many other forms of asset, setting motor vehicle RV's is relatively simple, because there is so much information published regarding trade sale values. Nevertheless, setting an RV still requires the Finance Company to take a substantial risk as to the likely value of the vehicle in a few years' time. That risk can be reduced by setting a low RV, thereby making it more likely that the net proceeds will be sufficient, but doing so will (for the reasons set out above) increase the rentals payable by the Customer and make the Finance Company's product less competitive in the market.

Lastly, as far as different types of hire agreement are concerned, it is worth noting that many of them incorporate an additional bundle of services which are to be provided by the Finance Company. Alongside the actual hire of the vehicle itself, the Customer is also provided with services in respect of other common elements relating to the possession and/or use of motor vehicles. Such arrangements typically involve the Finance Company paying for the maintenance and/or servicing of the vehicle, but this package of services can extend to other items as well, such as the replacement of tyres, the provision of relief vehicles, and accident management services.

These sorts of hire agreements, commonly known as 'contract hire', began as part of larger scale fleet business hire arrangements. More recently, though, changes in employee tax have reduced the benefits of 'company cars', which has led to a growth in the use of business car schemes which are based on arrangements direct between the Finance Company and individual employees, often (though not exclusively) based on contract hire structures. This in turn seems to have created an increasing willingness on the part of retail Customers to shift away from traditional ownership structures such as HP, towards structures based on possession and use only, such as personal contract hire (P.C.P.) agreements.

For obvious reasons, Finance Companies have a particular interest in ensuring that vehicles subject to hire agreements are properly looked after and maintained by Customers. This is so for all types of hire, given that the vehicle belongs to the Finance Company and represents a valuable asset which will need to be recovered and sold if the Customer defaults; however, it is particularly true for operating leases. To some extent, a Finance Company will have less of an interest in the residual value of a vehicle the end of the hire term when it is subject to a finance lease, given that nearly all of that value will end up being returned to the Customer when the vehicle is sold. On the other hand, if the vehicle is subject to an operating lease, the Finance Company has to take a genuine risk as regards the value of the vehicle at the end of the hire period. In the circumstances, it is particularly important for the Finance Company to ensure that the vehicle is returned in the right condition, so as to maximise the net sale proceeds which are achievable.

Accordingly, whilst all hire agreements contain provisions requiring Customers to use, look after, maintain and fully insure the vehicle during the hire term, operating leases contain extensive provisions (usually referred to as return conditions) detailing the state in which the vehicle must be on return, and making the Customer responsible for the cost of any work required to put it into the appropriate state of repair.

Otherwise, as for sale-based products, hire agreements typically contain provisions allowing the Finance Company to terminate the hiring of the vehicle in the event of default by the Customer, so that it can be recovered and sold, together with arrangements for the payment by the Customer of any shortfall suffered by the Finance Company once such sale has taken place.

Hire Purchase

Hire purchase is really a hybrid vehicle finance product. As the name suggests, it is both a hire agreement and a purchase agreement, in that the Customer agrees to hire the vehicle from the Finance Company and pay rentals during the hire period, but is also given an option to purchase it, usually once all the rentals have been paid. The payment structure can vary. Payment of part of the vehicle price by the Customer up front, in the form of a deposit (whether by way of cash or the trade in of an existing vehicle), is common, though not strictly necessary. It is also normal for standard retail hire purchase products to assist Customers with budgeting for the regular payments by adopting what is known as a 'flat' payment structure, with all the rentals being equal. However, the rental structure can in theory be whatever the Finance Company and the Customer agree, and it is common in business hire purchase for there to be reduced rentals through the hire term, with a much larger final rental (referred to as a 'balloon' rental) at the end. These forms of agreement are often referred to as 'contract purchase'.

Until a few years ago, the vast majority of motor vehicle hire purchase agreements were, in reality, indistinguishable from conditional sale agreements. Technically, the legal form of contract is different, but in both conditional sale and standard HP agreements, the Customer is obliged to repay the full cost of the vehicle, plus the Finance Company's charges, through the rentals come what may. In a conditional sale agreement, the transfer of title following the completion of the repayments is automatic, whereas an HP agreement does require the exercise of an option by the Customer before title will transfer. Nevertheless, it has long been recognised that it is economically unlikely that a Customer would pay the full value of a vehicle running into many thousands of pounds, and all the Finance Company's charges, but then decide not to pay a nominal purchase fee in order to become the owner of the vehicle at the end of the hire period. In practice, therefore, there is really little genuine chance that a standard HP agreement will not result in the transfer of title to the Customer if all rentals are paid.

The position is very different for the form of hire purchase usually referred to as personal contract purchase, or PCP. Although not new, this structure has become increasingly popular with retail Customers over the last few years. It is important to remember that a PCP agreement is just another form of hire purchase. However, PCP is arguably the only true form of hire purchase current in the motor vehicle finance market, in that at the end of the hire term there is a genuine option decision for the Customer to take. A standard HP agreement is a full pay out structure; effectively, it is a finance lease with an option to purchase tagged onto the end. On the other hand, a contract purchase agreement is not a full pay out structure; effectively, it is an operating lease with an option for the Customer to purchase the vehicle at the end of the hire period by paying the Finance Company the RV (often referred to as the Guaranteed Minimum Price, or GMP).

Whether or not the Customer decides to exercise that option will, in practice, depend on whether the actual market value of the vehicle at the end of the hire period is more or less than the GMP. If the Customer decides to exercise the option, then the final balloon rental is payable and the Customer becomes the owner of the vehicle. On the other hand, if the Customer does not exercise their option, then as long as the vehicle is in accordance with the return conditions, it will go back to the Finance Company for sale in the same way as under an operating lease, and the Customer pays no more.

The essential benefits of a P.C.P. structure for a Customer are again similar to those inherent in an operating lease. Deferral of the payment of the RV element of the initial cost of the vehicle until the end of the hire period reduces the interim rentals payable, and the option puts the risk on the Finance Company as to whether the actual value of the vehicle at the end of the hire term is more or less than the anticipated RV. The potential disadvantages of PCP are less often appreciated by Customers. Firstly, because payment of a large proportion of the value of the vehicle is deferred until the end of the hire period, the finance charges payable overall can be higher in contrast to standard HP. Secondly, if the Customer decides to walk away at the end of the hire period without exercising the option, they will have no trade-in value to put towards the purchase of a replacement vehicle (and may actually have lost the trade-in value that they put into the P.C.P. contract at the beginning of the arrangement).

In the same way as for hire agreements, all hire purchase agreements will necessarily contain provisions relating to the protection of the vehicle's value during the hire period, for termination of the hiring in the event that repossession becomes necessary, and for payment of any shortfall remaining after the vehicle is sold in order. In addition, in much the same way as for operating leases, PCP agreements will contain extensive return conditions designed to protect the Finance Company's position on resale if the vehicle is returned by the Customer at the end of the hire period.

CHAPTER FIVE
GENERAL COMPLIANCE

No consideration of compliance and regulation, however high level, would be complete without some reference to two other subjects which are core to any to motor finance transaction; Data Protection and Money Laundering. However, it must be emphasised that these are complex areas and the following summary is particularly high level.

Data Protection

This is an issue which often causes unnecessary problems for Sellers and Finance Companies, because it appears to be more complicated than it really is. There are of course detailed rules which are not always easy to apply, but as with much regulation, data protection is based on fairly straightforward principles; as ever, it is the details that tend to confuse.

The fundamental precept of Data Protection law is that people are entitled to their privacy. In a modern society, all sorts of information about people is shared and stored by a whole host of organisations for a variety of reasons. Data Protection law is intended to give people (in this context usually referred to as individuals or 'data subjects') rights against those organisations, and to ensure they have the information which they need in order to be able to enforce those rights.

Much ink has been spilled recently over the upgrade of Data Protection law contained in the GDPR, but as with other areas of compliance that apply to motor finance law, many of the changes introduced by the GDPR were actually designed to strengthen old law, rather than introduce new law. As such, many of the fundamental principles that have applied for many years remain unchanged.

Any data concerning a Data Subject is 'personal data', and any action taken in respect of personal data, including storing it, is referred to as 'processing'. Data Protection law does not apply to personal data processed by individuals about other individuals for social and domestic purposes. However, organisations that do things with personal data have to follow certain rules.

Such organisations fall into two categories. Most will be 'Data Controllers'; organisations which make their own decisions about what data they collect, how they deal with and store it, and what actions they take in regard to it.

The other type of organisation is a 'Data Processor', a concept that is much misunderstood. It does not simply mean that the organisation is processing personal data; Data Controllers process personal data. Rather, a Data Processor is an organisation that is not making its own choices about the data that it processes, but is doing so in accordance with the instructions of another organisation, which is the Data Controller for that particular data. The boundary between the two can be difficult to define, but essentially Data Processors are 'only obeying orders'.

The distinction is important, because Data Processors are subject to much less regulation, even after the introduction of the GDPR. They have duties, but essentially it is the Data Controller that is responsible for what the Data Processor does. For this reason, Data Processors need to act in accordance with a formal legal contract, but provided that they do so competently and without knowingly breaching Data Protection law, it will be the Data Controller that takes responsibility for the majority of issues that may arise.

The six principles that underpin Data Protection law can be summarised as:

- Personal data must only be processed in a manner that is lawful, fair and transparent;
- It must only be collected for specific, explicit and legitimate purposes, and must not be processed in a manner that is incompatible with those purposes;

- It must be limited to what is necessary for the intended purposes;
- The data must be accurate and up to date;
- The data must retained for no longer than is necessary for the specified purposes; and
- The data must be kept secure against unlawful processing or loss.

As indicated above, it is the Data Controller that is responsible for all of these things, and any processing that they (or a Data Processor on their behalf) undertakes will only be acceptable if carried out in accordance with one of the lawful justifications set out in the GDPR, of which those most relevant to Motor Finance law are:

- The Data Subject has given consent;
- The processing is necessary for the performance of a contract to which the data subject is party (which includes steps taken pre-contract);
- The Data Controller is under a legal obligation to engage in the processing; or
- The Data Controller has a 'legitimate interest' in the processing which is not overridden by the rights of the Data Subject.

Whenever a Data Controller comes into possession of personal data (either directly or because the data is collected by a Data Processor on their behalf), they are under a duty to inform the Data Subject. Clearly, no Data Subject can exercise their rights in respect of the data held by a Data Controller unless and until they have the necessary information; not least, of course, the fact that the Data Controller has got the data.

Essentially, a Data Controller can come into possession of data in two ways: they can obtain it directly from the Data Subject, or from a third party. The details of, and timing within which, this information needs to be given varies, but essentially the Data Controller needs to inform the Data Subject of:

- The identity and contact details of the Data Controller;
- The intended purposes of processing, and the legal basis on which the Data Controller relies;
- What data is being held;
- How long the data will be kept;
- If relevant, details of the Controller's 'legitimate interest' for processing the data;
- The right of the Data Subject to withdraw consent for processing (if that is the basis on which the Data Controller relies);
- The Data Subject's rights to request details of the data held, to require rectification or erasure, or to restrict or object to processing;
- The Data Subject's right to lodge a complaint with the Information Commissioner's Office; and
- Details of any automated decision-making that may take place.

Full details of the rights of the Data Subject, including the right to make a Subject Access Request, are outside the scope of this book, but it is worth highlighting the need for all organisations involved in the processing of personal data to:

- Identify exactly what data they control;

- Analyse the basis on which they process that data;
- inform the Data Subject appropriately; and
- ensure that they are taking the necessary steps to protect that data.

Information for data subjects is often given in the form of a written notice, but can be done verbally. Such notifications are usually referred to as being the Data Controller's 'fair processing notice' or 'privacy policy'. Neither name has any particular legal implications; all that is really important is that the necessary information is given.

If a Data Controller obtains the information directly from the data subject, then the information needs to be given there and then. On the other hand, if the information comes from a third party, the requirement is for the relevant information to be given as soon as reasonably practicable, but in no less than thirty days.

Where contact between the data subject and the data controller takes place at a distance (perhaps via the internet or e-mail), this does not prevent it being direct for data protection purposes. However, the involvement of intermediaries within the Motor Finance market, such as dealers or brokers, is often misunderstood, and does require proper analysis of each party's data protection status, and the relevant 'data flows'.

By way of example of such analysis, take the position of a motor dealer Seller with high street premises. The Customer will enter the premises and engage with the Seller, who will almost certainly want to gather information about the Customer and store it for its own future purposes, even if no finance is involved. In this case, the Seller is clearly acting as a Data Controller, and will need to give the Customer a fair processing notice. The Seller may obtain some of its data about the Customer from third parties, but since at least some will come direct from the Customer, this notice must be given there and then.

Such notices need to include details of any third party to which the Seller intends to pass some or all of the data it collects. Clearly, if any proposal for finance is being contemplated, the Finance Company will be such a third party. In such circumstances, it is likely that there is a contractual arrangement between the Seller and the Finance Company, under which the Seller is entitled to put forward such proposals on behalf of Customers for the Finance Company to consider, and to receive a commission payment if this introduction results in a completed finance agreement. However, the fact that such a contract exists does not mean that the Seller is doing any data processing under the control of the Finance Company; neither does it mean that the Finance Company, when it considers its response to the proposal, is processing data under the control of the Seller. Each of them is acting independently, and each will be a distinct Data Controller in respect of such of the Customer's personal data as they receive.

From the Finance Company's point of view, this data will come from various sources; some will be contained in the proposal; other data will come from the Finance Company's own records and from searches carried out with credit reference and/or fraud prevention agencies. In any event, the Finance Company is acting as a Data Controller and needs to ensure that the Customer has received a fair processing notice explaining all the necessary things which it, the Finance Company, needs to explain. The Finance Company could provide the Customer with that fair processing notice directly; more often, though, it will arrange for the Seller to do this on its behalf. Since all of the data will have been collected from third parties rather than from the data subject directly, the Finance Company could take up to thirty days to comply, but again in practice will tend to make sure this is done up front. Either way, though, as the transaction progresses the Customer will need to receive two distinct fair processing notices; one from the Seller and one from the Finance Company.

It is standard practice for Finance Companies to limit this initial fair processing notice to the steps which they will be taking in respect of the consideration of, and response to, the proposal. This will then, if the Customer does enter into an agreement, be consolidated by a further and rather lengthier fair processing notice, which details the additional processing which will or may take place thereafter; in particular, the collection of the payments that fall due, which may include the provision of data to third parties such as collection agents and credit reference agencies.

Finance Companies will also need to deal with a wider range of issues relating to personal data that they obtain and store, including subject access requests, but such detail lies outside the scope of this book. However, as a final point, passing mention should be made that there are special rules that apply to the use of personal data for marketing purposes; in particular, where such marketing takes place by electronic means.

Money Laundering

Increasingly complicated rules have been introduced over the past few years as part of ongoing attempts by governments around the world to deal with the financial elements of terrorist funding and other criminal activity. Essentially, terrorists and other criminals who want to hide the fact that the funds they are spending have been obtained by dubious or 'dirty' means, need to treat them in such a way as to make them appear legitimate or 'clean'. The steps in this process are usually described as:

- Placement – introducing the dirty funds into the legitimate financial world;
- Layering – moving those funds around in order to hide their source; and
- Integration – taking the funds back out so they can be spent as 'clean' money

Such 'laundering' can take place in a number of ways, and the scope of the Money Laundering Regulations 2017, and other associated legislation, is complex. Essentially, though, from the point of view of motor vehicle finance, there is an obligation on most participants in the market to take conscious steps to minimise the ability for their business activities to be used for the purposes of money laundering, which broadly involves the firm in:

- taking conscious steps to assess the risks of their particular business activities being misused for money laundering

- developing practices and procedures which minimise those risks;

- having a proper understanding of who their customers are, why they are engaged in a given transaction, and where their funds come from; and

- making sure that suspicious activity is identified and reported to the relevant authorities.

Essential guidance on how to deal with these issues can be found in the JMLSG (Joint Money Laundering Steering Group) Guidance. This guidance supports the view that motor vehicle finance is broadly a low risk area of activity, but that doesn't mean it is 'no risk'. Accordingly, all participants will need to be able to demonstrate that they take active measures to address that risk, such as it is, and to further minimise it.

The core of such measures will be checking the identification of Customers and those linked with them, such as directors and controllers, and the identification of potentially suspicious transactions. There are also particular rules that must be addressed regarding individuals and/or organisations who may be subject to international sanction, or who may simply be what are referred to as 'Politically Exposed Persons' or PEPs. These are people whose political connections mean that they are potentially more likely to come into contact with dirty money. On the subject of PEPs, people usually think of politicians from third world countries where corruption and the like are supposedly more commonplace. In reality, though, such illegal activities are far from limited in this geographic way, so neither are the rules on PEPs.

In any event, as with any other area of regulation, full risk analysis needs to be made and appropriate measures put in place. In one sense, taking the right steps to try to minimise money laundering is almost more important than actually doing so. Transactions involving money laundering will inevitably occur; that is recognised by governments and regulators alike. What is important is that the 'innocent' parties involved in such transactions have taken reasonable steps to try to avoid money laundering taking place. If they have done so, they will not be blamed simply because it transpires that the transaction was misused. On the other hand, if they do not take appropriate steps to try to minimise money laundering, they will be blamed and can be fined substantially, even if no money laundering has actually taken place.

CHAPTER SIX
GETTING IN BUSINESS

All Finance Companies need to obtain business, and there are various ways in which they can do so. In the Motor Vehicle finance market, the most common forms are:

- advertising, either direct or through an intermediary; or
- Introduction by an intermediary, such as a dealer or broker.

Looking first at intermediaries, such introductions are commonplace, but do not create any particular issues in general law. Sometimes questions of 'agency' arise; in other words, whether a particular party to the transaction was in some way acting at some stage on behalf of another party. Generally, though, this is not the case. As mentioned elsewhere, it has long been accepted by the courts as a matter of general law that unless actually appointed as an agent by a Finance Company, or specifically held out in some way by the Finance Company as being so appointed, neither a Seller nor any other finance broker will be treated as being an agent of the Finance Company. Similar considerations apply to the relationship between Sellers and Customers, and the fact that an intermediary submits a proposal to a Finance Company on behalf of a Customer, does not of itself mean that they are acting as the Customer's agent. In the vast majority of cases, therefore, the Customer, the Seller and the Finance Company are all acting in their own right, and questions of general agency do not often arise.

One exception to this general rule may be referred to as 'branded' intermediaries; those who are for one reason or another treated as being an integral part of the Finance Company's wider organisation. There are, however, very limited circumstances in which an intermediary is seen as being held out by the Finance Company to a Customer as being authorised to state and/or agree things on its behalf. Even where a motor vehicle manufacturer both owns a Finance Company and franchises a Seller to use the manufacturers brand to market its vehicles, there is still normally sufficient distinction between the Finance Company and the Seller to avoid such agency issues.

It is, of course, for exactly this reason that the 1974 Act provided in section 56 that in certain cases, the Seller would be treated as if it were acting as an agent of the Finance company when engaged in anything which could be seen as part of the negotiations leading to the making of a regulated credit agreement. This provision will apply to retail motor vehicle finance credit based transactions, and even to business purpose credit agreements if they are regulated. However, it must always be remembered that the section 56 deemed agency does not apply to unregulated agreements; neither does it apply to hire agreements, whether regulated or unregulated.

Advertising

Another common way for Finance Companies to obtain business is to advertise, either directly themselves or through an intermediary. Even at general law, there are significant restrictions on the approach to advertising that can be adopted. The Advertising Standards Authority is technically a form of self-regulation by the advertising industry rather than an independent regulator, but it does in practice have considerable power to ensure that advertising is not misleading. In addition, there are general regulations in place to protect consumers from unfair or aggressive business practices, which would extend to cover any advertising by Finance Companies or by Sellers (whether on behalf of the Finance Company on their own behalf). There are even regulations to protect businesses from the misleading marketing activities of other businesses. As such, there is quite a body of law which is generally aimed at ensuring that advertising and other marketing activities are conducted in an acceptable manner.

Beyond this, any firm authorised by the FCA is under an obligation to ensure that its 'financial promotions' are 'clear, fair and not misleading'. A financial promotion includes an advertisement, but goes much further. Advertisements are publications which require a wider audience, but the concept of financial promotion extends to cover almost any communication between an authorised firm and a Customer in respect of an actual or potential financial transaction. Furthermore, engaging in the financial promotion of a regulated product without either being authorised by the FCA or doing so using materials approved by an authorised firm, is a criminal offence.

Lastly, in this regard, there are specific and somewhat arcane rules applying to consumer credit advertising. It is not meant as a criticism to say that the dark arts of advertising inevitably involve highlighting the benefits of a product, whilst at the same time not putting potential Customers off by mentioning the disadvantages that may be involved, whether they be general or relate only to a particular class of Customer. The FCA's 'clear, fair and not misleading' requirements address this issue in a generic manner. However, the FCA also inherited a consumer credit regime that dealt with the issue in a different manner. Accordingly, we still have both the generic approach and specific CCA requirements.

As mentioned many times in this book, consumer credit regulation is often designed to ensure that consumers are able to make informed decisions. In the context of advertising, this is not possible unless the information that they are given is not only correct, but also complete. In its most simple form, there are no special requirements that an advertiser must comply with, save to ensure that the Customer is informed of the identity of the advertiser in question. Accordingly, advertisements which consist of little more than statements to the effect of 'we give people finance' are not subject to any detailed rules.

It is when Finance Companies or other advertisers start to take certain steps to more actively promote regulated credit products that they need to comply with detailed rules designed to prevent them doing so in a manner that is overly partial. In particular, as soon as they start to make specific suggestions about the quality of, and/or the benefits to be obtained from, entering into the potential finance arrangement, they need to make the Customer aware of the potential cost involved. This is done by requiring the advertiser to quote a 'typical APR' in order to give the Customer some idea of the total charges that may be involved. A typical APR is an APR which the advertiser has good reason to expect will be available to at least 51% of the intended target audience for the advertisement. The vehicle or the finance product may be advertised with headline benefits designed to tempt the unwary, but if the APR is high it may cause some to think twice about the deal.

Likewise, if the advertisement contains certain items of specific financial information about the finance product, such as the level of repayments to be made, it needs to do so as part of a 'typical example' which contains a full range of relevant information, including of course an indication of the total cost to the Customer of taking out the advertised credit. There are also prominence rules which require the advertiser to ensure that the less attractive elements of this information, such as the costs involved, are given at least equal billing with those elements which are designed to incentivise the Customer to take the credit out

For these reasons, consumer credit advertisers need to take particular care in order to ensure that the technicalities of the CCA advertising rules are met. Those rules do not apply to hire agreement; nor do they apply to advertisements which are clearly directed only to business Customers. Nevertheless, advertisers of such products will in practice need to take similar levels of care to ensure that their products are being promoted in a manner that is 'clear, fair and not misleading'

Brokers

As indicated elsewhere, all FCA authorised firms need to be able to demonstrate, if so required, that they are well set up, financially sound and competent to carry out the activities that they have permission to engage in. This applies as much to the activities of credit brokers, including Sellers, as to any other authorised firm. However, there are also special rules requiring credit brokers to provide certain relevant information to Customers.

Essentially, these rules require the credit broker to make it clear:

- that they will be acting as an intermediary, rather than the actual provider of the finance; and

- that if the Customer's application for finance is successful, the credit broker will receive payment from the Finance Company for making the introduction.

The FCA considers remuneration to be a particularly important element of any financial transaction, in that otherwise perfectly acceptable market activities can be distorted by the way in which the parties to a transaction are remunerated. To take a simple example, a credit broker may be offered different levels of commission by two Finance Companies. It would obviously be in the commercial interests of the credit broker to place the business with the Finance Company that will pay the highest level of commission, but it may be in the Customer's best interests to enter into an agreement on the terms available from the other Finance Company. How is this issue to be reconciled?

The FCA does have general rules regarding conflicts of interest and the way in which firms are required to deal with them. In addition, though, credit brokers are required to ensure that the Customer is made aware they will be paid commission by the Finance Company as part of the transaction. Unlike some other areas of financial regulation, this requirement does not extend to formal disclosure of the amount of commission involved. Only if specifically asked by the customer is the credit broker required to disclose this information.

CHAPTER SEVEN
PRE-CONTRACT REQUIREMENTS

The requirements for CCA documentation are quite extensive. However, before the parties to an agreement get anywhere close to the signature stage, there are a number of important issues that need to be dealt with by the Finance Company. As explained elsewhere, this area of motor vehicle finance law has become somewhat fragmented, not least by the changes needed to comply with the CCD.

Dealing therefore firstly with the position as it applies to agreements that falls within CCD scope, the Finance Company needs to:

- assess the Customer's 'creditworthiness';
- provide the Customer with an 'adequate explanation' of certain required features of the credit; and
- provide the Customer with 'pre-contract information' in a specified format.

A creditworthiness assessment needs to be based on 'sufficient information'; this includes not only information already known to the Finance Company, but also such additional information as may be reasonably necessary to make the required assessment, as obtained from the Customer and/or a credit reference agency.

The exact application of these requirements is a matter for each Finance Company to consider. As such, there is no hard and fast methodology for a creditworthiness assessment. It is also true that a failure to comply properly with this requirement will not directly impact on the enforceability of the relevant credit agreement in the same way as other breaches of the 1974 Act requirements. On the other hand, Finance Companies are now not only required to take reasonable steps to carry out such assessments properly, but also to document each individual assessment. Accordingly, any general failure to comply would be a regulatory issue which could lead to the Finance Company being required by the FCA to engage in a remediation exercise in respect of affected customers, which would undoubtedly involve the payment of some level of compensation to those who would not have satisfied a proper assessment process. Furthermore, a failure to adequately document an individual assessment could lead to a substantial number of Customer complaints and even claims for compensation, whether conducted through the FOS or as part of claims management company activity.

In addition to assessing creditworthiness, before the parties enter into the proposed credit agreement, the Finance Company has to ensure that the Customer has (directly or via a credit intermediary) been provided with an adequate explanation of the following matters:

- any potential unsuitability of the finance for the Customer's purposes;
- any adverse features of the finance agreement which might not be obvious to the Customer;
- details of the payments due;
- the potential consequences of non-payment; and
- the Customer's rights of withdrawal (if any), and how to exercise them.

At the same time as giving the adequate explanation, the Finance Company is also required to inform the customer:

- that they should consider the pre-contract information that they will be given, and can take it away;
- that they have the opportunity to ask questions;
- how they can get further information; and

- whether or not they are entitled to a copy of the draft agreement.

Of course, whether a given explanation is, or is not, adequate can be hard to judge. Again, both objective and subjective factors will apply. The explanation clearly has to be one that any reasonable Customer is likely to understand, but the Finance Company also needs to be able to demonstrate that it has taken reasonable steps to ensure that a given Customer has in fact understood it. This will involve the Finance Company setting up a process to ensure not only that each Customer is given an explanation which the Finance Company is reasonably entitled to regard as adequate for that Customer, but also designed to pick up any obvious lack of understanding. Such a process may also need to vary between different types of Customer, depending on their likely experience of finance arrangements.

One thing the Finance Company cannot do, however, is to get the Customer to confirm that the explanation given was 'adequate'. The Customer can be asked to confirm that they have received a particular explanation, but it always up to the Finance Company to prove, if needs be, that it was adequate. Anything else would be equivalent to the Customer signing away their consumer rights.

The method of providing the required explanation is to some extent prescribed. Essentially, the issues of potential unsuitability, payments due and withdrawal act as trigger points. If any of these items are explained to the Customer orally or in person, then the other issues (and the additional required information) must also be explained orally. In practice, what this means is that if the explanation is provided via post or over the internet, then it can be in writing; however, if it is provided over the telephone, or face to face, then it must be given orally.

As regards the timing for all this, it is in theory possible for the explanation to be given at any time, provided that it is prior to the making of the relevant agreement. Again, though, practical considerations make it inevitable that the explanation will be given as part of the process for the completion of the finance agreement, because no Finance Company is going to want to spend time and money giving such an explanation unless/until that stage has been reached.

As regards the Finance Company's duty to provide a Customer with a draft copy of the credit agreement, this will be the case unless the Finance Company is not at that stage willing to proceed to enter into the relevant agreement. This is fine in theory. However, since in practice Finance Companies will not usually be willing to do so unless/until the point of executing the proposed finance agreement, the provision is somewhat less helpful to Customers than it might at first appear.

The Consumer Credit (Disclosure of Information) Regulations 2010 requires Finance Companies intending to enter into agreements within CCD scope to disclose certain information to the Customer in advance. The information requirements are quite detailed, but are intended to ensure that the Customer is put in a position to make an informed decision about entry into the agreement. From a motor finance perspective, the requirements include:

- the type of credit;
- details of the Finance Company and the Seller;
- the amount of credit;
- the term of the agreement;
- the vehicle that the agreement relates to;
- the rate of interest chargeable;
- the APR;
- details of the amount, number and frequency of repayments;
- any other charges that may end up being paid by the Customer;
- any default charges and/or interest;

- a warning about the consequences of missing payment;
- the existence or absence of a right of withdrawal; and
- the Customer's right of early repayment.

The regulations also specify the form and manner of disclosure. It needs to be in the form of what is presently referred to as the 'Standard European Consumer Credit Information' sheet or SECCI (though this is due to be renamed in 2019). Further, it has to be both in writing and removable by the Customer, and the SECCI must only contain the required information.

As indicated already, the CCD does not apply to agreements for business purposes or where the credit exceeds the £60,260 limit. Accordingly, there is nothing in the CCD which would require Customers entering into such agreements to have their creditworthiness assessed or to be provided with an adequate explanation. Furthermore, there were no similar requirements applying under the 1974 Act prior to CCD implementation. That situation remains unchanged in respect of hire agreements, and what was CCA secured lending has now almost all been moved over to the mortgage regime.

However, when the CCD requirements were being implemented, some of the provisions were felt to be suitable for wider application. Accordingly:

- business purposes agreements were made subject to a requirement that the Customer must be given an adequate explanation; and
- the requirement for a creditworthiness assessment applies to both agreements for business purposes, and those where the credit exceeds £60,260.

In theory, therefore, there is no requirement for an adequate explanation to be given in respect of credit exceeding £60,260. Equally, there is no requirement for either an adequate explanation or a creditworthiness assessment where the Finance Company is intending to enter into a hire agreement. However, the position is not quite as simple as that. A Finance Company that enters into CCA regulated agreements requires to be authorised by the FCA. As explained elsewhere, the FCA general approach is to require authorised Firms to conduct the whole of their business in accordance with certain principles, not just the regulated part of their business. Those principles include the concept of TCF, and it is at least strongly arguable that it might be unfair for a Finance Company to treat two Customers differently for the purposes of creditworthiness and/or adequate explanations, when both are entering into motor vehicle finance agreements containing very similar obligations. HP and hire agreements may be legally different, but leaving aside the issue of title, the Customer is taking on responsibilities and financial obligations which are substantially the same. This being so, is it fair or reasonable for the Finance Company to deal with them in different ways? Accordingly, whilst Finance Companies are not currently subject to an express requirement to follow these CCD based provisions in all circumstances, it is strongly arguable that it would be advisable to adopt a similar approach to all Customers (including possibly even those whose agreements will be unregulated) as a matter of general principle.

In any event, whether or not the requirements for creditworthiness and/or adequate explanations should be applied to agreements outside CCD scope, there is certainly an equivalent requirement for the giving of pre-contract information in respect of such agreements. In this case, the Finance Company needs to comply with the requirements of the Consumer Credit (Disclosure of Information) Regulations 2004, though this is easy to do, in that;

- the information only needs be given to the Customer at some stage before the agreement is presented to them for signature; and

- these regulations require that the information to be given mirrors precisely the information which the relevant agreement is also required to contain.

In practice, therefore, for agreements outside CCD scope, the pre-contract information document is just a facsimile of the agreement itself, from the heading down to but not including the signature box, which the Customer will receive immediately before they receive a copy of the agreement itself. In the circumstances, it is hard to see that Customers will gain any more understanding from reading the pre-contract information than from reading the agreement itself, and they are no more likely to read either document than if they received the agreement alone. The SECCI suffers from the same timing issue, though it can be argued that whilst much the same information is required as is contained in the agreement, it is at least required to be set out in a different format. Either way, though, it is hard not to see this requirement for pre-contract information as being an exercise paid for ultimately by consumers which conveys no real benefits in practice.

CHAPTER EIGHT
FORM OF CONTRACT

As with any legal contract, certain requirements need to be satisfied; in particular, there needs to be a process of offer and acceptance, made in respect of a set of clear terms that are capable of forming a contract, by parties who are intending to create a binding and enforceable relationship. In the context of motor vehicle finance, the standard analysis is that the submission of proposals and the issue of acceptance terms are merely negotiations. Only when the agreed terms have been set out in writing and signed by the parties (or at the very least unequivocally acknowledged by them) can it be said that a contract has come into existence.

In general, contracts do not need to be either written down or signed in order to be enforceable and/or valid. Accordingly, with some important exceptions which we will come to shortly, there is no strict requirement that motor vehicle finance contracts need to be in writing. The reasons why they invariably are written down are almost entirely practical. Firstly, the parties need to know that the period of negotiation is over, and they have got to point of 'contract'. Secondly, there is always the possibility that the parties will have some form of disagreement over the terms of the contract, or otherwise need to confirm what was actually agreed between them.

This isn't so much about going to court, though doing so is clearly an occurrence that would require proper evidence of the contract terms to be produced. Rather, it's about not going to court; in that clear and unequivocal written terms will both minimise the chances of any dispute and, if needs be, allow the parties to avoid the expense of getting a judge to resolve their dispute by reminding each other (and themselves) as to what those agreed terms were.

As such, whilst not strictly required for most business contracts, it would be highly unusual for even B2B contracts not to be in writing.

Such contracts can appear to take a number of forms, but these all tend to be variations on two basic patterns:

- Single shot agreements, which may cover a number of vehicles, but are intended to be complete in themselves as regards the vehicles, rentals and other terms; and

- 'master' agreements, which set out core terms that will apply if and whenever the parties enter into any number of subsequent finance arrangements by completing a 'schedule', each of which will be distinct as regards the vehicles and rentals specified.

The length and complexity of both types of agreement can vary considerably. In the largest or most complex commercial transactions, the exact terms may need to be laboriously negotiated by the parties, but in general most motor vehicle finance agreements are written on standard 'vanilla' documents drafted by the Finance Companies themselves, which tend to contain similar clauses dealing with a range of standard issues, as highlighted in Chapter Four. These clauses are understandably concerned primarily with protecting the financial interests of the Finance Company which is, after all, the party to these arrangements which is taking the primary risk by advancing credit and/or giving over possession and use of its property to the Customer.

As regards signature, this is again more about evidencing the precise contract terms that have been agreed rather than a formal requirement. In the circumstances, whilst not commonplace, it is always open to the parties at common law to rely on a verbal contract rather than reducing the terms into writing, and/or to dispense with signature on one or both sides. Doing so does not necessarily invalidate the contract, but it does carry the risk of making the existence and/or terms of the contract less than clear.

There are, however, exceptions to this. The requirements of the 1974 Act regime are one example, but another must count as being amongst the earliest examples of consumer protection legislation. The Statute of Frauds 1677 still requires certain types of contract to be both in writing and signed, including a contract of guarantee. In the context of motor vehicle finance, this means that even if the finance agreement itself may not require this level of formality, any guarantee by a third-party individual regarding the Customer's performance of the contract does.

Generally, the contents of any contract are primarily a matter of negotiation between the parties, who are fundamentally free to agree such terms as they think fit. However, that general position is in practice subject to increasing levels of oversight and interference by Regulators; not so much for commercial transactions, but very much where consumers are involved. Finance Companies nearly always transact motor vehicle finance on the basis of standard terms. As a result, such agreements are subject to the requirements of 'unfair contract terms' legislation. In particular, a Finance Company may not attempt to exclude or restrict liability in respect of the main implied terms such as quality, fitness for purpose, delivery and risk (of which, see more in Chapter X below) in a consumer agreement, and can only do so even in a business agreement if it is 'reasonable'.

This is not always simply a matter of the Finance Company being precluded from putting a general term to that effect into the contract. Terms are also not permitted if they purport to indirectly limit a consumer Customer's rights in respect of the implied terms by:

- excluding or restricting a particular right or remedy;
- making such a right or remedy subject to restrictive or onerous conditions;
- putting the Customer at a disadvantage when it comes to pursuing their rights or remedies; or
- attempting to exclude or restrict the way in which rules of evidence or procedure will apply to a claim.

More generally, all the terms of a consumer finance agreement will need to satisfy the 'unfair terms test'. The vehicle itself and the price payable by the Customer are outside that test, provided that all of the relevant information on those points is expressed in a plain and intelligible manner, and is brought to the Customer's attention in such a way that an average consumer would be aware of it. In practice, it would be unusual for a finance agreement regulated by the 1974 Act not to be in compliance with these requirements. In most cases, therefore, the main application of the unfair terms test will be to the additional standard 'terms and conditions' which are part of the finance agreement. It is also, for obvious reasons, not possible for a consumer to contract out of these statutory protections.

The unfair terms test involves looking at whether a particular term creates a significant imbalance in the respective rights and obligations of the contract parties, to the detriment of the consumer, and in breach of the requirements of good faith. When looking at a term, a court (or other regulator) would take into account the subject matter of the contract, the other contract terms, and all of the other circumstances. Essentially, when drafting its standard terms, a Finance Company needs to strike a fair balance between its own genuine commercial interests and those of its consumer Customers, so that it provides itself with reasonable protection without undue impact on the rights of consumers. It may be noted that this requirement is very similar to the FCA's concept of 'treating customers fairly', and indeed the FCA has responsibility for the oversight of unfair terms law within the financial services market.

It needs to be appreciated that this process is not limited to looking at the wording of an individual term in isolation. The long-held position of the OFT, as adopted by the FCA when it took on the oversight of unfair terms for financial services agreements, is that a clause may appear innocuous in its own right, but still carry the potential for misuse. For example, a clause that excludes the implied terms but states that consumer rights are not affected is arguably not breach of the CRA, but nevertheless has obvious potential to mislead consumers.

In addition, the language used in drafting consumer contracts needs to be understandable by ordinary people, not just by lawyers. This prohibits the use of wording that has have been honed to a precise meaning over many court disputes, such as 'indemnify', in favour of more general wording such as 'compensate for loss suffered'. However, whilst this might create a level of uncertainty, it is certainly much more easily understood by Customers, and as we have seen the general trend of consumer protection regulation is to ensure that Customers are able to make informed decisions. Also, as regards the interpretation of unfair terms, it is worth noting that if a term is capable of having more than one interpretation, it must be construed in a manner that is in favour of a consumer Customer, rather than the Finance Company.

If a term is held to be unfair, it will not be binding on a consumer Customer. As such, the Customer may rely on it if they wish, but the Finance Company may not. On the other hand, the rest of the contract will be unaffected, and still may be relied on by the Finance Company. In particular, no permission is required for the contract to be enforced, provided the unfair term is not being relied on.

The fairness of terms can be raised by a consumer as an issue in any claim relating to the contract; in the context of motor vehicle finance, this means that a term can be put in question during any dispute between the Customer and the Finance Company, whether or not that dispute even involves the term. Furthermore, whenever any consumer contract is in front of a court, the judge is under a duty to consider the fairness of its terms, even if the point has not been raised by the parties themselves. Strictly this should not happen unless the court has been provided with sufficient material for it to be able to reach a proper judgment on the issue, which would in most cases require the parties to have prepared and put forward arguments on the point. However, it is always a possibility that must be taken into account.

Finally, it should be noted that all this will in practice require a Finance Company to either maintain separate sets of terms for business and consumer use, or to deal with all its customers on a single set of terms which would be acceptable in a consumer context. It is still in theory possible to draft a single set of terms that would operate differently for business and consumer transactions. In practice, though, this approach has considerable risks. Apart from anything else, the FCA approach is that terms will be unfair if they are reasonably capable of being misunderstood by, or misrepresented to, the average consumer, notwithstanding that they may be perfectly clear to a specialist contract lawyer.

CHAPTER NINE
CCA DOCUMENTATION

The other major exception to the rule that contracts don't need to be in writing is, of course, when a Customer is entering into a 1974 Act regulated agreement. Section 61(1) states that a regulated agreement is not properly executed unless a document in the prescribed form, containing all the prescribed terms and conforming to the relevant regulations is signed by both the Customer and the Finance Company. In addition, that document must embody all of the terms of the agreement, other than implied terms, and must comply with various requirements as to legibility.

As will be readily apparent, these requirements are designed to do two things:

- Ensure that the Customer is fully aware in advance of the nature and extent of the contractual obligations they will be taking on, so that they can make an informed decision about whether to do so; and

- Formally record the parties' entry into the contract, and its exact terms, so as to minimise the potential for misunderstanding and subsequent dispute.

Of course, these aims are not always achieved. Customers cannot be physically forced to read the contract terms before signing, and even if the terms of a contract are clearly set out there can still be scope for different interpretations. However, whilst far from perfect in operation, the documentation and execution provisions set out in the 1974 Act are rightly regarded as a crucial part of consumer protection. As a result, the consequences of a failure by a Finance Company to ensure compliance with those provisions are substantial. Section 60 says that if the documentation and execution requirements have not been followed properly, the agreement will be unenforceable without a court order.

A number of practical points can be made regarding these requirements:

- Complying with the documentation requirements is easier said than done, given the complexity of the relevant regulations, so there is always potential for an inadvertent breach. Accordingly, it is essential that the Finance Company can always demonstrate that it has tried its best to comply with the spirit of the requirements, to avoid being held culpable for the breach;

- If a breach does occur, it does not invalidate an affected agreement, so that if the Customer continues to comply with it, for example by making payments, then the Finance Company is under no obligation to highlight the issue. It is only once the Customer ceases to comply, and the question of potential enforcement arises, that the Finance Company may become obliged to inform the customer about the fact of unenforceability;

- As set out elsewhere, the Finance Company is entitled to take reasonable steps to move the Customer through the required processes leading, if necessary, to the issue of an application to the court for an enforcement order. However, such an application is not required in every case, because the Customer can at any stage accede to the Finance Company's requirements, usually by making payment and/or returning the vehicle.

Essentially, a Finance Company is entitled to take reasonable steps to require a Customer to comply with the terms of an 'unenforceable' agreement, but must deal with the Customer fairly by ensuring that they are properly informed about their rights and the consequences of non-compliance.

Assuming that the Finance Company has complied with all the relevant pre-contractual requirements, it is then entitled to move on to the completion of the finance agreement itself. As already mentioned, the introduction of the CCD has created a fragmented approach to documentation requirements, which requires CCD and non-CCD agreements to be dealt with in very different ways.

Starting with CCD scope agreement, the form and content requirements are set out in the Consumer Credit (Agreements) Regulations 2010 (the 2010 Regulations). These set out in some detail the financial and related particulars which the agreement is required to contain. These are understandably much the same as those required for the SECCI, which have already been detailed elsewhere. The 2010 Regulations also set out the statements of protection and remedies that the Customer needs to be provided with, including:

- their rights of redress if the vehicle is not up to standard;
- their right to early termination of an HP or conditional sale agreement;
- how to complain to the FOS; and
- the existence of the FCA as regulator.

This information needs to be set out in writing in a document in a manner that is 'clear and concise'. The document then needs to be signed by both parties, but there is no requirement for the Customer to do so within a special signature box.

As will be appreciated, these requirements are not hugely technical, and can be quite flexible in practice; unfortunately, the same cannot be said of the requirements applying to agreements outside CCD scope. The Consumer Credit (Agreements) Regulations 1983 (the 1983 Regulations) set out the requirements which govern the form and content of hire agreements and those credit agreements which fall outside CCD. These regulations are in many ways similar to the 2010 Regulations, in that both require similar information to be given, along with statutory statements of protections and remedies. However, the 1983 Regulations are much more prescriptive as to how this needs to be done. Rather than simply being required to be set out in a manner that is 'clear and concise', the required information and statements have to be given under the following headings:

- Key Financial Information (for both credit and hire agreements);

- Other Financial Information (for credit agreements only); and

- Key Information (for both credit and hire agreements).

The 1983 Regulations set out in detail what prescribed information must appear under which heading; in addition, they require that this information must not only be shown together as a whole, but must not be preceded by, or interspersed with, any other information. Some of the provisions in these regulations are notoriously difficult to apply in practice. Furthermore, the prescribed information and the order in which it has to be set out, and the wording of the prescribed statements, leave much to be desired.

In the circumstances, it is far from easy for Finance Companies to be confident that they are in compliance with the 1983 Regulations, no matter how hard they may be trying. What is worse, since compliance is a matter of following the regulations precisely, it can be difficult to find ways to make an agreement more comprehensible for the Customer. Be that as it may, the required information again needs to be set out in writing in a document, which then needs to be signed by both parties; under the 1983 Regulations, however, it is a requirement for the Customer to do so within a special signature box.

Lastly on the subject of documentation, a word about electronic documents. As originally drafted, the 1974 Act required hard copy documents. However, between them, section 176A of the 1974 Act and the Consumer Credit (Electronic Communications) Regulations 2004 were introduced to permit regulated CCA transactions to be completed by electronic means. This extends to both simple email transmission of documents, and to more complicated arrangements for online completion, including electronic signatures.

In one sense, the various requirements of the 1974 Act and the relevant regulations are unchanged. For a regulated agreement to be properly executed, the Finance Company still needs to provide copies of 'documents' containing the necessary information and statements, with the agreement 'document' being signed; what has changed is only the permitted method for achieving this. In other words, the Finance Company has to have a process which achieves by electronic means exactly what would happen if the agreement were hard copy. Verifiable signatures need to be made, and copies need to be 'given' in a form that can be retained for future reference. Strictly, the Customer needs to agree to this approach, but in practice that will always be academic, in that if they are not happy (or able) to do so, the agreement will simply never come into existence.

This modern electronic approach broadly applies nowadays throughout CCA compliance, with most required notices and documentation capable of being validly given to Customers by electronic means. It is, though, worth remembering that are exceptions; for example, a section 87 Default Notice can be emailed to a Customer for information purposes, but must still be sent by post or delivered personally if it is to have any effect.

Finally, therefore, having ensured that the documentation is in the right form the Finance Company can move on to the formal execution of the agreement itself. The requirements of the 1974 Act on this subject are not always obvious at first sight, and have unfortunately become increasingly difficult to interpret as new requirements have been introduced. The fact that both parties need to sign is straightforward enough. What in practice tends to cause confusion is the different requirements for copies of the agreement to be provided, which itself depends on how the agreement is presented for signature, and when it becomes an 'executed' (that is, binding) contract. Accordingly, before moving into the detail, it is helpful to start from basics by looking at the background reasons for the requirements, starting with the way in which regulated motor vehicle finance agreements tended to be executed in the 1970s, when the original requirements were designed.

At the time, there were a number of alternative ways in which such documentation could be signed up, but for reasons explained elsewhere, a combination of the popularity of credit based finance and the provisions relating to the post-execution cancellation of regulated credit agreements, meant that in the vast majority of cases the execution process involved the Finance Company sending the documentation in paper form to the Seller, who would then present it to the Customer for signature on the Seller's premises Although it was possible for the agreement to be pre-signed by the Finance Company, so that it would become an executed agreement as soon as the Customer signed, this was unusual in the 1970s. Accordingly, once the Customer had signed, the original copy of the agreement would be returned to the Finance Company, usually by post, so that it might conduct final checks before signing itself in order to bring the agreement into force.

Since this was so, it was clearly important that the Customer was provided at the time of signing with a copy of the agreement that they had offered to enter into. The execution provisions therefore required that whenever an agreement did not become final and binding when the Customer signed, they must be given an 'unexecuted copy'. This would allow them to understand the potential obligations that they had offered to take on and, since the contract would not be final and binding until signed by the Finance Company as well, give them a last opportunity to withdraw that offer.

Assuming, though, that the Customer did not withdraw, it was also clearly important that they should know when those obligations had become fully binding; in other words, when the agreement had been signed by the Finance Company. This issue was addressed by requiring the Finance Company to send an 'executed copy' of the agreement to the Customer within seven days after it had itself signed.

Although less common, a similar process would apply if the agreement was sent to the Customer by post. Once signed by the Customer, it would be returned for the Finance Company to sign. Accordingly, at the same time as the Customer was sent the original to sign, they needed to be sent an 'unexecuted copy' to keep for reference. Likewise, after the Finance Company had signed, an 'executed copy' needed to be sent out.

As mentioned above, it was unusual at the time for a motor finance agreement to be pre-signed by the Finance Company. However, such arrangements were not uncommon in respect of other types of regulated finance, and the 1974 Act did provide for execution in this manner. In such cases, the agreement becomes fully executed when signed by the Customer. Accordingly, there is no need for them to be given an 'unexecuted copy' at the time; all that is required is for the Customer to be provided with an 'executed copy' for future reference, whether the agreement has been presented to them in person or sent by post. This being so, there is no need for them to be sent a further 'executed copy' later on, save in the case of cancellable agreements (which are dealt with in the next chapter).

Once the practicalities are taken into account, the provisions of the 1974 Act dealing with execution and the provision of copies become, if not clear, at least more understandable. Unfortunately, these execution arrangements have been further complicated by the introduction of the CCD. The original execution requirements at least had the benefit of applying to all CCA regulated agreements. Now, however, there are alternative approaches which need to be applied according to whether the relevant agreement falls inside or outside CCD scope, with the added complication that a Finance Company can in certain circumstances adopt the CCD approach in respect of a credit agreement that is actually outside CCD scope.

The first point to remember is that the CCD has no application to hire agreements, which can only be documented and executed using the old style CCA requirements. However, for those agreements which are within CCD scope, there is no longer any strict need to serve an 'unexecuted copy' at all; the only requirement is that once the agreement has become executed, whether on the signature of the Customer or the Finance Company, an 'executed copy' must be given to the Customer. That said, 'unexecuted copies' are still relevant in practice, because the new requirements go on to provide that an 'executed copy' does not need to be provided by the Finance Company if the Customer has already been given an 'unexecuted copy'. Where this is the case, the Creditor is instead required to confirm to the Customer that the agreement has been executed in identical form, and that the Customer has a right to ask for an 'executed copy' within the 14-day period allowed for withdrawal (see below).

The new CCD approach to execution is really just another way of dealing with the same issues as the old CCA approach is designed to address. The lack of any strict requirement to serve an unexecuted copy creates no particular detriment to Customers, given that CCD scope agreements come with an unfettered right of post execution withdrawal which is built round the provision of a copy (whether executed or unexecuted). In practice, though, having two parallel regimes is unhelpful, not least because the practice of providing Customers with unexecuted copies continues and it is not unusual for an executed copy to be sent out after a Finance Company has signed, on a 'belt and braces' approach. There is nothing wrong in this, provided that the Finance Company remembers that complying with the old-style practice is no substitute for complying with the CCD scope requirements. Failure to do so would mean that the agreement had not been properly executed, and was therefore unenforceable.

One final point should be noted regarding the provision of copies of an agreement. Whilst it may be common practice for Finance Companies to do so, the regulations made under the 1974 Act make it clear that they are not under an obligation to provide a Customer with a facsimile copy of the agreement as signed. Rather, the obligation is to provide what is in banking terms referred to as a 'true copy', in which all relevant information is set out, but certain things are allowed to be omitted; in particular, the parties' signatures. As such, it has been confirmed by the courts that a Finance Company is perfectly entitled to reconstitute a regulated agreement from information within its possession in order to provide the Customer with a 'statutory copy'; it is not required to produce a facsimile copy of the actual agreement which was executed by the Customer.

CHAPTER TEN
CANCELLATION AND WITHDRAWAL

For obvious reasons, the execution of regulated agreements is inextricably linked with the concepts of cancellation and withdrawal. The basic principle underlying this area of regulation is relatively simple. There is no common law right for a party to a contract to decide that they have changed their mind and would like to be released from their obligations, and accordingly no general right for commercial Customers to cancel or withdraw. However, for consumer protection reasons, it has been decided by Regulators that in appropriate circumstances, once an agreement has been executed, a Customer should be given a 'cooling off period' in which to decide whether they do really wish to be bound by the obligations that they have signed up to. It can be important to remember that any statutory right of 'withdrawal' is not the same thing as the withdrawal of an offer to enter into an agreement before that offer has been accepted by the other party. Under general contract law, any offer can be withdrawn up to the point at which the agreement becomes executed. Statutory rights of cancellation and withdrawal, however, only apply in respect of executed agreements.

Unfortunately, as with a number of other areas of motor finance law, there are a number of different consumer rights that may apply to an agreement, and the interaction between them is not always clear and consistent. This inevitably causes confusion, but again unpeeling the various layers to appreciate each in isolation before looking at how the layers interact can assist understanding.

There are essentially three distinct cooling off periods which can apply:

- CCA 'cancellation' under section 67 of the 1974 Act;

- The CCD right of 'withdrawal', as set out in section 66A of the 1974 Act; and

- consumer finance contracts can also have a right of 'distance cancellation'.

Section 67 is a general right which applies to both credit and hire agreements, though for technical reasons set below, it is less common in respect of hire. Distance cancellation also applies to both, though via different mechanisms; credit agreements are dealt with through the EU Distance Marketing Directive, as currently set out in the FCA Handbook, but for hire agreements it is via the Consumer Contracts (Information, Cancellation and Additional Charges) Regulations 2013.

More than one of these cooling off periods could apply to a given agreement, but there are rules designed to prevent this happening in most circumstances. Section 67 and the right of distance cancellation are dis-applied if the agreement is subject to section 66A, and as the requirements for section 67 involve face to face negotiations, distance cancellation and section 67 are by definition mutually exclusive. Finance Companies do sometimes utilise forms of documentation which incorporate both section 67 and distance cancellation rights, but this is usually for commercial reasons.

Distance contracts are dealt with elsewhere in this book, but consideration needs to be given here to the way in which sections 67 and 66A apply, and the important differences in the effect each can have. It makes sense to start with section 67 as the underlying 'old style' right, but before doing so consideration needs to be given to section 56 which defines the important 1974 Act concept of 'antecedent negotiations'.

Essentially, these are any discussions taking place in the run up to the making of a regulated agreement between the Customer and a defined 'negotiator', being either the Finance Company itself or:

- a credit broker, if the discussions lead to the making of a hire purchase or conditional sale agreement; or

- any Seller, if that Seller and the Finance Company are connected by pre-existing arrangements so that the discussions lead to the making of a connected lender loan agreement.

The reason why the definition of antecedent negotiations in section 56 is so important to the consideration of section 67 cancellation, is that the section only applies if there are 'antecedent negotiations' which include oral representations made by the negotiator in the presence of the Customer. What this means in the context of motor vehicle finance is that section 67 cancellation will most often only apply to credit agreements, because any face to face negotiations leading to the making of a motor vehicle finance agreement will almost invariably be conducted by an intermediary of some sort, rather than by the Finance Company itself. This being so, the definition of 'antecedent negotiations' will only be satisfied in respect of a hire agreement if conducted directly by the Finance Company itself, or by its appointed agent. Absent such agency, the definition will not be satisfied if the negotiations are conducted by a Seller or other intermediary, because such intermediaries will only be a 'negotiator' under section 56 if the end agreement is one of credit. Accordingly, unless there is an actual agency in place between the Finance Company and the Seller/credit broker, which would be unusual, negotiations conducted by intermediaries leading to the making of a hire agreement will not relevant for the purposes of section 67.

Assuming, though, that there are in fact 'antecedent negotiations' of some sort, and the technical requirements for the representations to be both oral and face to face are satisfied, then the agreement will be cancellable under section 67 unless it is signed by the Customer on premises at which either the Finance Company or the negotiator are carrying on business; these are usually referred to as 'trade premises'. It used to be commonplace for Finance Companies to insist that all regulated motor vehicle finance agreements were signed on 'trade premises', so as to avoid the application of section 67. This was partly because complying with section 67 is a complex process in itself, but mainly because the effect on the Finance Company if the cancellation right is exercised can be quite severe.

Looking firstly at compliance, if section 67 applies, the Finance Company is required to provide the Customer with three forms of cancellation notice. Firstly, the original agreement must itself contain a form of notice which does no more than inform the Customer that the agreement is cancellable and that they will be provided with further details by the Finance Company. The Customer must then be provided with a second, slightly longer, notice, which explains that the Finance Company will be in touch to provide details as to how and when the cancellation right can be exercised. This notice must form part of a statutory copy of, and be given to the Customer at the same time as they sign, the agreement. If at that point the agreement becomes fully executed, then the notice must go in the 'executed copy'; alternatively, the notice goes in the 'unexecuted copy'.

Lastly, a third notice must be sent separately by the Finance Company to the Customer once the agreement has become executed. If the agreement does not become executed when the Customer signs, then the notice must be incorporated into the 'executed copy' which is sent when the Finance Company signs. Alternatively, if the agreement does become executed when the Customer signs, so that the 'executed copy' is given at that stage rather than sent later on, a separate notice must be sent by the Finance Company within the usual seven-day period. In either case, the third notice will confirm to the Customer that they can cancel the agreement by giving notice in writing within five days after receiving the notice. The Finance Company must at the same time provide the Customer with a statutory cancellation form to use for this purpose, but the Customer is not required to use the form unless they wish to do so.

As indicated above, if a Customer does exercise a section 67 cancellation right, the effect for the Finance Company can be severe. The agreement is to be treated as if never made, which in this context means that the finance arrangements are unwound, the vehicle will be returned to the Finance Company and the Customer is entitled to recover all payments they may have made, as well as being released from future payments. Essentially, provided the vehicle is returned in an acceptable condition, the Customer is entitled to walk away as if the agreement had never been entered into, leaving the Finance Company holding a used vehicle which is potentially worth rather less than the price which it paid for the vehicle only a few days previously when the finance agreement was set up. It is little wonder that Finance Companies went to great lengths to ensure that retail motor vehicle credit agreements were signed on 'trade premises'.

As we shall see, though, the overall effect of section 66A is rather different from that of section 67. The withdrawal right itself is of much wider application, in that if section 66A applies the Customer is entitled to withdraw from the agreement, without giving any reason whatsoever, within a fourteen-day period. There are technical rules as to when this period begins, but normally in practice it will be when the Customer either signs, if the agreement then becomes executed, or receives a later notice of execution by the Finance Company. As indicated, section 66A does apply to business purpose regulated agreements, but does not apply if the credit exceeds the CCD scope limit of £60,260.

However, although the scope of section 66A is much wider than section 67, the end result of 'withdrawal' is nowhere near as severe for the Finance Company. When the possible introduction of the withdrawal right which eventually became section 66A was first suggested by the European Parliament, many Finance Companies were very concerned, because they assumed that the effect of withdrawal would be similar to that which applies in respect of section 67. That has, however, turned out not to be the case.

It is true that if the right of withdrawal is exercised, the agreement is in theory treated as if it was never entered into. However, section 66A incorporates a statutory requirement that the Customer has to repay the credit that they have been given within 30 days, together with interest at a stated contract rate. Unlike section 67, therefore, section 66A does not entitle the Customer to effectively avoid responsibility for their decision to enter into the finance agreement. The Customer may be entitled to withdraw from the finance arrangement which has been set up to fund their purchase of the vehicle, but is effectively still bound to purchase the vehicle by other means.

If the Customer does repay the credit under a hire purchase or conditional sale agreement, then section 66A provides that they will become the owner of the vehicle. However, if the Customer does not repay, then the Finance Company is entitled to pursue repayment of both the credit and interest at a daily rate as a statutory debt. Furthermore, whilst not explicitly stated in section 66A, it must follow that the Finance Company, as the owner of the vehicle, will be entitled to repossess and sell it, and to use the net proceeds to reduce (though not necessarily extinguish) the statutory debt. As a result, whilst the Customer may in theory have an unfettered right to withdraw under section 66A, they are unlikely to do so unless they are able to repay the Finance Company.

Finally in this section, a word on the scope of section 66A. Rather unhelpfully, it does not only apply to agreements that are within CCD scope; it was also extended by the UK government to cover regulated business purpose agreements, which are strictly outside CCD scope. On the other hand, credit agreements exceeding the CCD value limit of £60,260 are not covered by section 66A. As with many 1974 Act rights, a Finance Company may voluntarily extend the scope of section 66A to agreements above the CCD value limit; there can be good commercial reasons for doing so rather than utilising multiple forms of documentation. However, it is important to remember that doing so will not operate to exclude section 67.

CHAPTER ELEVEN
POST-CONTRACT DISPUTES

Once the formalities of the finance agreement are out of the way, all the parties would clearly hope that matters will now proceed smoothly. Unfortunately, this is the point at which practical problems often intervene, most usually in connection with one or both of two factors:

- The condition of the vehicle, and/or its suitability for the purposes that the Customer intends to use it for; and
- any representations made by the Seller which turn out to be incorrect or untrue.

The basic common law position is very much 'buyer beware'. In pure contract theory, the parties should be free to negotiate exactly what terms they wish to have in their agreement, so if the Customer wants to be sure that the vehicle will meet a certain standard, it is up to the Customer to negotiate a contract containing a clause in which the Finance Company promises that this will be so. Of course, things are not that simple in practice, not least because this theory leaves the Finance Company equally free to ensure that the contract contains a clause saying it has no responsibility for the condition of the vehicle. Given that motor finance agreements are by and large drafted by the Finance Company and presented to the Customer on a 'take it or leave it' basis, this leaves the Customer in a difficult position.

This is particularly true for consumers, who tend to have little or no negotiating power in such circumstances, but even business Customers will almost certainly have no choice but to enter into motor finance agreements that have been drafted in advance by the Finance Company, rather than negotiated individually with the Customer. As a result, and as already seen, in this area of motor finance law the protections afforded to Customers are not limited to consumers; some of the more fundamental ones apply also to business contracts. Unfortunately, as is so often the case, the landscape is rather fragmented, which can lead to confusion.

It is therefore perhaps easiest to start with business contracts. There have since the late nineteenth century been statutory terms implied into all contracts for the sale of goods. In respect of business contracts, the latest versions of these terms are contained in the Sale of Goods Act 1979, and equivalent terms are also implied into other types of contract for the supply of motor vehicles; by the Supply of Goods (Implied Terms) Act 1973 in respect of HP, and by the Supply of Goods & Services Act 1982 in respect of hire.

Most motor vehicle finance agreements will be for HP or hire, but it is essential to remember that in such circumstances the Finance Company will be the 'supplier' of the vehicle to the Customer, not the Seller. The Seller will have supplied the vehicle to the Finance Company under a contract of sale, which will also contain the same implied terms. As such, whilst it is in practice almost always the Seller that will ultimately be responsible for sorting out any issues with the vehicle, it is important to remember that under this chain of liability, it is the Finance Company that is primarily responsible to the Customer. For this reason, in this section use will be made of the expression 'supplier', which can encompass both a Seller and/or a Finance Company, depending on context.

All of these statutes work in much the same way, in that the vehicle needs to comply with a number of implied terms. There are terms relating to the rights of the Customer to have uninterrupted possession and/or use of the vehicle during the currency of the agreement and (if appropriate) for the Finance Company to pass title to the Customer. More particularly, there are terms as to fitness and quality, including:

- The vehicle supplied must be consistent with any contractual description. This will normally just be a matter of stating the make, model and registration number, but the description may also extend to any additional items that were intended to be supplied with, or fitted to, the vehicle.

- The vehicle must be of satisfactory quality, which means it must meet the standard that a reasonable person would regard as satisfactory, taking into account the description, the price payable by the Customer, and all other relevant circumstances. The quality of goods includes their general state and condition; their fitness for the purposes for which such vehicles are commonly supplied; their appearance and finish; and their safety, durability and freedom from minor defects. The implied term does not extend to any aspect of the vehicle which might make it unsatisfactory, if that aspect is specifically drawn to the Customer's attention in advance, or is something that an actual examination of the vehicle carried out by the Customer should have revealed.

- Lastly, in addition to the requirement for fitness for general use that is implied into the definition of satisfactory quality, there is a further implied term that the goods must be fit for any particular purpose which the Customer expressly or impliedly makes known to the supplier. This term does not apply where the circumstances show that the Customer did not in fact rely on the supplier when deciding whether the goods were fit for the purpose, or that it would for some reason be unreasonable for him to have done so.

In practice, deciding whether a vehicle is up to standard or not, is a question of reasonable judgement. The standard of condition required for a second-hand vehicle would inevitably be somewhat lower than that for a new one; a car with defects would still be up to standard if they were declared and the price was right; even a written off vehicle would be of satisfactory quality if sold for scrap. The right approach is to look at the contract and the surrounding circumstances in order to decide on the appropriate standard for the particular vehicle to meet, and then to look at the vehicle itself to decide whether it does so or not.

In theory, therefore, every business contract for the finance of a motor vehicle could include these implied terms relating to the condition and quality of the vehicle, and any breach by the supplier would entitle the Customer to claim damages to compensate for the loss suffered.

However, such terms are regarded as being so fundamental to the contract, that in the case of substantial breach the Customer will also have the alternative remedy of terminating the contract altogether, by 'rejecting' the vehicle as unfit and reclaiming any money paid. It may be helpful at this stage to clarify one common misconception regarding this process. From a legal point of view, it is the party in breach which has 'repudiated' the contract; the innocent party then 'accepts' that repudiation by rejecting the vehicle.

To add to the complexity of such disputes, claims under the contract that the vehicle is not of the right quality, or somehow does not satisfy the Customer's expectations, often require detailed consideration of who said what to whom, and whether that statement had some legal effect. An obvious example would be whether the Customer had engaged in any discussions with the supplier regarding any special purpose for which they intended to use the vehicle, but any process for the supply of a motor vehicle will inevitably involve discussions that are bound to include statements or 'representations' regarding its capabilities. Sometimes, a Customer will have little or no contact with the Finance Company, but most such disputes do involve direct discussions between them and the Seller. That inevitably brings up the question of whether the Finance Company, in its capacity as the supplier of the vehicle, is responsible for things said and done by the Seller during discussions to which the Finance Company was not party and may know nothing about. This involves looking carefully at two legal issues:

- did any statement made by or to the Seller during those discussions become incorporated into the terms of the finance contract, or otherwise be something for which the Finance Company needs to accept responsibility?

- Alternatively, might any misrepresentation by the Seller be the subject of a direct claim by the Customer?

This is a particularly complex area, which is well outside the scope of this book. In brief, though, in a B2B context, the discussions between the Customer and the Seller are something for which a Finance

Company will have little or no responsibility. The courts have long accepted that unless a Seller is expressly held out by a Finance Company as being its agent, there will be no implied agency; furthermore, the fact that a Seller may have a relationship with a Finance Company which enables it to set up finance arrangements for the Customer is not in itself sufficient to imply that any agency exists. In other words, in the absence of any actual agency (which would be unusual), claims or other representations made by the Seller in advance of the finance contract will not become part of the finance contract or otherwise be binding on the Finance Company; they will be something that needs to be dealt with direct between the Customer and the Seller.

Unfortunately for the Customer, such direct claims against a Seller are far from easy to pursue. It is perfectly possible for there to be an additional (collateral) contract direct between the Seller and the Customer. However, unless there is a clearly agreed contract document, it can be hard for a Customer to argue that their general discussions with the Seller were capable of satisfying all the required elements of a binding contract. Another alternative would be a claim for misrepresentation, but again there would a number of technical points which the Customer would struggle to satisfy: that there was a statement of fact, as opposed to opinion; that the statement was false in some material way; that the Customer placed reliance on it, and that the Customer has somehow suffered a specific detriment as a result. As such, direct claims against the Seller by the Customer can in practice be very difficult to establish.

Returning then for the moment to the standard contractual position, it is the case that terms regarding quality are in theory implied into all motor vehicle finance contracts. However, in a business context, whether or not a particular agreement does contain such terms is often less clear, and depends on the circumstances of the particular transaction. As we will see, there is one crucial difference between consumer and business contracts; namely, that the implied terms can never be excluded or limited in a consumer contract. By contrast, business contracts can contain clauses, usually just referred to as 'exclusion clauses', which are intended to exclude and/or limit the effect of these implied terms.

Clearly, as mentioned briefly above, any Finance Company is going to wish to exclude the implied terms if it is able to do so, not least because it is really only providing a financial service, and will in practice almost never have had any direct physical contact with the vehicle. The Finance Company may in many cases purchase ownership of the vehicle from the Seller in order to enter into the finance agreement, but as we have seen, possession and use will be granted to the Customer, who will almost always take delivery of the vehicle direct from the Seller. In practice, whether the Finance Company is able to successfully exclude the implied terms will depend on the provisions of the Unfair Contract Terms Act 1977 (UCTA).

In brief, UCTA provides that a party to a business contract cannot exclude or restrict its liability under a contract, or otherwise use the terms of the contract to render a performance substantially different from that which was anticipated, unless the relevant contract terms satisfy a requirement of reasonableness. Whether such a term is reasonable is to be decided with regard to all the circumstances which were, or which reasonably ought to have been known to the parties at the time they made the contract. This is all somewhat vague, and deliberately so in order to leave the courts free to interpret the provision in a flexible manner. However, UCTA does set out some guidelines for the application of the test, including:

- the relative bargaining positions of the parties;
- whether there was any benefit to the Customer in agreeing the term;
- whether the Customer in fact knew or ought to have known of the existence of the term; and
- whether the goods were manufactured to the Customer's order.

None of these guidelines are hard and fast, and they are not intended to limit the general nature of the test of reasonableness. However, in the context of a motor vehicle finance contract, a Finance Company would usually argue that it should be entitled to exclude responsibility for the vehicle condition because:

- it is really only providing the Customer with a financial service;
- it only purchased the vehicle for that purpose and at the request of the Customer;
- the vehicle has been supplied by a Seller chosen by the Customer themselves;
- the pricing for the agreement is based on the premise that the Finance Company does not take such responsibility; and
- it would have been both possible and entirely reasonable for the Customer to obtain enforceable assurances regarding the vehicle condition and quality direct from the Seller.

In the circumstances, it is normal practice for a Finance Company to ensure that the agreement contains relevant exclusion clauses, which are always worded so as to maximise the prospect for arguing that they are reasonable. Finance Companies do recognise, though, that these clauses are not 100% effective; in fact, as a matter of risk analysis it is probably best to regard them as being somewhere in the region of 50% effective. In other words, they may or may not work in the context of a given dispute, but they are worth having in the agreement, and must certainly be relied on if the matter does go to court.

Of course, even if a problem with the vehicle does arise, the parties would generally look to resolve it between themselves, rather than allow it to escalate into a full-blown dispute. It is for this reason that it should always be remembered (but is all too often forgotten) that whilst the arrangements for the provision of a practical solution to the dispute will nearly always be discussed direct between the Seller and the Customer, it is the Finance Company that is the supplier of the vehicle and contractually liable for its condition. Of course, the Seller is still contractually liable, just not to the Customer; rather, the Seller is contractually to the Finance Company. In theory then, if the vehicle is not satisfactory for the purposes of the finance agreement, it must also not be satisfactory for the purposes of the sale agreement.

Accordingly, if the matter does need to go to court for the dispute to be resolved, the right approach would be for the Customer to issue proceedings against the Finance Company as supplier, who would defend on the basis that the allegations of breach are not accepted, but in the event that they are valid, the Finance Company is entitled to rely on the exclusion clauses. In turn, the Finance Company would then issue a third-party claim against the Seller, effectively saying that if the Finance Company is liable to the Customer, then the Seller must be equally liable to the Finance Company. The Seller will presumably put forward its grounds for denying the validity of the Customer's allegations of breach of the implied terms. In this way, the Finance Company acts the legal conduit for the dispute to be argued out between the Customer and the Seller, with the Finance Company passing responsibility up and down the line as necessary.

Of course, any Finance Company will work hard not to allow the matter to get to this stage. It may well be possible as part of any court proceedings for the Finance Company to claim for the balance due under the finance agreement. Furthermore, if the Customer's claim is upheld then the Seller would have to compensate the Finance Company, and if the Customer's claim is not upheld the Customer will have to pay. However, any reasonable business organisation will want to avoid both the cost and the risk involved in such litigation. Accordingly, in such circumstances, Finance Companies go to great lengths to keep the Customer 'in the vehicle' and paying under the finance agreement. Indeed, from a Finance Company point of view, one of the practical problems involved in dealing with such disputes is that because the Customer and the Seller engage directly, those parties may have irrevocably fallen out long before the Finance Company even learns of the existence of the dispute. This can in practice make it difficult for the

Finance Company to move the process forward towards a reasonable settlement.

As explained, whilst business Customers do in theory have the benefit of implied terms relating to quality and fitness for purpose of vehicles supplied, those terms can be, and often are, excluded. In addition, there are often practical problems in the enforcement of those rights, and in dealing with any non-contractual issues that may arise out of the behaviour of the Seller prior to the setting up of the various agreements. Business Customers are not entirely unprotected, but for obvious reasons it has long been felt that consumers need to have far more protection. The current protections afforded to them are now to be found in the Consumer Rights Act 2015 ("CRA").

As an initial point, it is important to remember that in this context, a consumer is an individual within the normal meaning of that word; someone who is entering into the relevant finance agreement for purposes which are wholly or mainly outside the realms of any business that they may operate. Clearly, the vast majority of ordinary retail Customers will fall within this definition, although there can be borderline cases. However, it must be remembered that whilst some business purpose agreements may be regulated by the 1974 Act, this will not mean that that the relevant Customers obtain consumer status for any purposes outside that regime.

The CRA was intended to both consolidate and reform large parts of UK consumer law, particularly as regards the rights and remedies for defective goods, and the way in which the law on unfair terms and consumer contracts worked. However, it is important to remember (certainly in the context of motor vehicle finance) that a large proportion of the provisions set out in the CRA were concerned less with granting consumers entirely new rights, and more with trying to ensure that the rights which consumers already had under the existing legislation could be properly enforced. In the circumstances, much of the pre-existing legislation, whilst now repealed, is still in force in another guise, so that the long history of court decisions regarding the interpretation and application of the implied terms is still entirely relevant.

The CRA was intended to cover all supplies of goods. Accordingly, in addition to sales contracts, including those which may contain any condition as to the transfer of title, it also applies to hire purchase and hire agreements. This has the benefit for Customers and Finance Companies of bringing all the relevant legislation in respect of consumer contracts under one regime, rather than being split between three different (albeit very similar) regimes, as it still is for business contracts.

Essentially, the CRA starts by repeating all of the pre-existing standards applicable to the supply of goods under those previous regimes, including those relating to the description, satisfactory quality and fitness for purpose of the vehicle, as set out above in respect of business contracts. In addition, though, the CRA introduces a number of new implied terms into consumer contracts. There is now a requirement that the vehicle has to remain at the risk of the Finance Company until the point at which it has been delivered to the Customer; in addition, that such delivery must take place without undue delay, and in any event within thirty days unless agreed otherwise. This last point does not, of course, mean that delivery cannot take place outside the thirty-day period. Rather, it means, that whenever a finance agreement is entered into in respect of a vehicle which is going to be delivered at some future point, that an extended delivery period needs to be agreed with the Customer as part of the agreement. Furthermore, that delivery period will need to be realistic, as a failure to comply would be a breach entitling the Customer to terminate the contract.

Under the CRA, it is assumed that a vehicle was not 'in conformity with the contract' at the date of supply (in other words, there has been a breach of the implied terms as to quality and fitness) if it is not in conformity at any point during the first six months after supply. Really, this provision is all about the burden of proof. If the Customer can show that the vehicle is not up to the required standard within the first six months, then it will be assumed that the relevant issue dated back to the point of supply, unless the supplier can prove otherwise. After the six-month period is over, the Customer does not lose any rights, but it is inherently less likely that any problems which are encountered would date back to the point of supply. Accordingly, matters revert to the standard contract law position, in that it will be up to the Customer to demonstrate that any current problems were in existence at the date of supply; not an impossible task, depending on how fundamental the problems are, but increasingly difficult as time passes.

It is, though, when it comes to the remedies for any breach of the implied terms as to quality and fitness for purpose, that the impact of the CRA is most felt. As we have seen, unless excluded of course, the implied terms as to quality and fitness for purpose will entitle even a business Customer to terminate and reject if they are breached by the Finance Company (in its capacity as the supplier of the vehicle). However, it is commonplace for there to be discussions, sometimes quite lengthy discussions, regarding the nature of the breach and whether it can be remedied by the Seller (in its capacity as the ultimate supplier). This is understandable, given that all the parties will in most cases want to reach a position where the vehicle is satisfactory to the Customer, and the finance agreement can continue.

The problem with this in practice is that as a matter of general contract law, a Customer is able to waive their right to reject the vehicle, and indicate that they wish instead to rely solely on a claim for damages. In theory, there is no reason why the parties cannot agree that the right to reject will merely be held in suspense while the parties explore the possibilities for the repair and/or replacement of the vehicle. Unfortunately, it was in practice not uncommon for Customers to find that by engaging in discussions about repair or replacement, they either had, or were at the very least being told by an unscrupulous Seller that they had, lost the right to reject. It was also sometimes difficult for Customers to place any restrictions on the number or timing of attempts by the supplier to repair or replace. All of this meant that such discussions were somewhat of a minefield for consumers.

The CRA did away with these issues by creating a statutory process for the consumer. Now, if the vehicle does not conform to the contract terms, the Customer has a number of specific rights:

- a short-term right to reject;

- a right to the repair or replacement of the vehicle;
- a right to a price reduction; and
- a final right to reject.

It is the way in which these rights interact that allows a Customer to access their rights, but at the same time safeguards the genuine commercial interests of the supplier. The key element in achieving this balance is the Customer's two rights of rejection.

Firstly, there is a short-term right, which needs to be exercised in the context of motor vehicle finance within thirty days after the delivery of the vehicle. This right to reject is unrestricted. The supplier (technically the Finance Company, but almost always in practice the Seller) can request an opportunity to repair or replace the vehicle, but cannot insist on doing so. Accordingly, if the Customer wants to reject, then the supplier has no option but to unwind the contract. However, in order to give the Customer the option to discuss the possibilities for the repair or replacement of the vehicle within this period, such discussions with the supplier automatically stop the clock, and the thirty day rejection period goes on hold for a prescribed 'waiting' period. This period begins when the Customer requests or agrees to repair or replacement, and ends when:

- the supplier either returns the vehicle as having been repaired or provides a replacement; or
- it becomes clear that the supplier will be unable to do so, or cannot do so within a reasonable time or without causing the Customer significant inconvenience.

If this happens, the new time limit for exercising the short-term right to reject will then be:

- the original time limit for exercising that right plus the waiting period; or

- if later, seven days after the waiting period ends.

This dual mechanism is intended to ensure that the Customer gets at least 7 days after the end of the waiting period to take a decision. By way of example, if a waiting period of 4 days ends on day 14 of the original rejection period, then the short term right to reject will expire on day 34 (30 plus 4); however, if the same waiting period ends on day 29, then the right to reject will instead expire on day 36 (29 plus 7) rather than day 34.

As indicated, if the Customer does opt to allow the supplier to repair or replace the vehicle, then the supplier must do so within a reasonable time, and without significant inconvenience to the Customer; it must also bear all of the costs involved. If the supplier fails to do so in line with these requirements, the Customer can still exercise the short term right to reject within the extended period. On the other hand, if the Customer does give the supplier a chance to repair or replace the vehicle, they cannot change their mind; as long as there is no significant inconvenience to the Customer (which in practice usually means the supplier needs to provide a short term replacement for the vehicle), they must allow the supplier a reasonable period in which to sort out the issue, and if the supplier is able to do so, the Customer must accept the vehicle back and continue with the finance contract.

In practice, many issues regarding the quality and fitness of vehicles will come up within this initial thirty day period, and will need to be dealt with in accordance with the short-term right to reject, and the suspension of this right to allow for any arrangement to effect repairs to, or replacement of, the vehicle. However, even once this thirty day period has expired, and the short-term right to reject has been lost, that is not the end of the story; as always, the essential question in such disputes is whether the vehicle was 'in conformity' with the contract at the date of supply.

If it was not, the Customer still has their rights of repair/replacement, price reduction and long-term rejection. On the other hand, once the short-term right to reject has been lost, the Customer is effectively required to allow the supplier an opportunity to repair or replace the vehicle because they are only entitled to opt for a price reduction and/or final rejection if:

- the supplier has made one attempt at repair or replacement, but the vehicle still does not conform to the contract; or
- the supplier cannot repair or replace the vehicle because it would be impossible or disproportionate for them to do so; or
- the Customer has required the supplier to repair or replace the vehicle, but the supplier has failed to do so within a reasonable time and/or without significant inconvenience to the Customer.

Only if one of these circumstances applies will the Customer then be entitled to a price reduction or to exercise their final right to reject.

If the Customer is entitled to exercise a final right to reject, then the CRA does allow a deduction to be made to take account of use for certain types of goods, but this does not apply in respect of a motor vehicle within the six-month period after delivery. In such circumstances, the supplier would need to take the vehicle back on an 'as is' basis.

As a final point, it needs to be remembered that whilst the finance agreement with the Customer will be governed by the CRA, the sale agreement between the Seller and the Finance Company will not; it will be governed by the old-style rules still applying to business contracts under the Sale of Goods Act 1979 and UCTA. In theory, this means that the Seller could validly exclude liability under the sale contract, whilst the Finance Company would be unable to do so under the finance agreement.

In practice, that is an unlikely scenario. For a start, it would be unusual for a Finance Company to purchase a vehicle on the Seller's terms; if any terms are agreed, they are normally going to be those of the Finance Company. Furthermore, even if the Seller's terms were applicable, it would still be a struggle to argue that excluding liability was reasonable. In most cases, therefore, the Seller is likely to be liable to compensate the Finance Company if and to the extent that it is itself liable to the Customer.

That said, a Finance Company needs to be very aware that being the supplier of a complex and expensive product carries a considerable risk of being dragged into potentially expensive disputes. This is true of any vehicle finance transaction, but the risk of the finance company being left substantially out of pocket is all the greater in consumer transactions. As such, any Finance Company would be well advised to take positive steps to ensure not only that it is contractually able to pass any such losses back to its Sellers (as the original supplier), but that those Sellers are going to be able pay.

Moving on then from implied contract terms to other issues arising from the behaviour of the Seller. As already mentioned, it was felt when the 1974 Act was being prepared that Finance Companies which received business referrals from a Seller ought to take some level of responsibility for wrongful behaviour by the Seller in connection with the underlying transaction that was being financed. This led to the introduction of a number of elements in the 1974 Act relating to this issue, in particular sections 56 and 75.

Essentially, these sections set out to address two broad issues set out at the start of this chapter:

- The condition of the vehicle, and/or its suitability for the purposes that the Customer intends to use it for; and

- any representations made by the Seller which turn out to be incorrect or untrue.

Representations made by the Seller to the Customer in order to induce them to enter into the transaction which turn out to be substantially incorrect are often referred to as 'misrepresentations'. These misrepresentations may relate to the vehicle, but may also relate to the finance arrangements themselves. In addition, there can be problems caused by any failure on the part of the Seller to comply with the terms of the contract for the supply of the vehicle, most often by breach of the implied terms relating to quality and fitness.

Misrepresentations by the Seller may be innocently made rather than deliberate, but either way the Customer is adversely affected and deserves protection. We have already seen in the context of section 67 cancellation that section 56 works by setting up a concept of 'antecedent negotiations'. In this context, section 56 goes on to provide that such negotiations are deemed to have been conducted by the Seller as an agent for the Finance Company.

It is worth making the point again that antecedent negotiations (and therefore the whole structure set up by section 56) have little relevance as far as hire agreements are concerned. Under the definition in section 56, the only circumstances in which there are 'antecedent negotiations' in connection with a prospective hire agreement, is when those negotiations are carried out by the Finance Company itself, or by a duly appointed agent of the Finance Company. As indicated elsewhere, it is unusual for Sellers or other intermediaries to be either appointed by Finance Companies as agents, or to be held out as being so.

Accordingly, the real effects of section 56 are in relation to credit agreements. The general position in respect of finance agreements is that because Sellers and other intermediaries are not agents of the Finance Company, the Finance Company is not responsible for any statements that they may make. This position is effectively reversed if section 56 applies, in that any representations made as part of the antecedent negotiations will be deemed to have been made by the Seller as agent for the Finance Company. This will be the case whether the Finance Company ends up being the supplier of the vehicle to the Customer (as in an HP or conditional sale agreement), or simply advances funds for the Customer to purchase the vehicle (as in a Motorloan). In either case, there is taken to be sufficient connection between the Finance Company and the Seller, as to make it reasonable for the Finance Company to take responsibility as if the Seller were an appointed agent.

It does need to be remembered that this does not mean the Seller is in fact the Finance Company's agent in general terms or for all purposes; it is only deemed to be so for the purposes of the antecedent negotiations. Nevertheless, section 56 is of wide application. The concept of antecedent negotiations is construed to include not only discussions regarding the finance agreement and the vehicle, but extends also to any peripheral matters that are part of the wider 'Customer transaction'. The most common example of this is in respect of a Seller undertaking to discharge finance due in respect of a Customer's trade-in vehicle; because of the deemed agency, if the Seller fails to do so, the Finance Company will need to arrange for this to be done.

Essentially, though, section 56 is addressing the issue of misrepresentations made by the Seller which directly or indirectly induce the Customer to enter into the finance agreement. Section 56 is not dealing with contractual breaches. Apart from anything else, when the finance agreement involves the supply of the vehicle by the Finance Company itself, such as in agreements of hire, hire purchase or conditional sale, the Finance Company is directly liable to the Customer for any issues regarding the vehicle. It is only where the Finance Company is not directly liable to the Customer in this way, as in a Motorloan, that is there any need for a mechanism to ensure that the Finance Company is liable for breaches of the supply contract by the Seller.

This issue is addressed by section 75. This provides that where the Finance Company and the Seller are connected by virtue of 'pre-existing arrangements', and the Customer has a claim against the Seller for misrepresentation or breach of contract, then the Customer has a 'like claim' against the Finance Company. If section 75 applies, the Customer is entitled to bring a claim direct against the Finance Company as if it had itself supplied the vehicle and/or made the relevant representation, with the Finance Company then having a statutory right of compensation from the Seller.

The coverage provided by section 75 is not unlimited. It would not apply if the cash price of the vehicle were less than £100, though that is obviously unlikely to be the case in practice; more relevantly, it does not apply if the cash price exceeds £30,000. It should, though, be noted that if section 75 does apply, the amount of credit that may have been given is irrelevant; the Finance Company is liable for the full amount of the Customer's claim, regardless of the amount of money that it may have advanced.

One further complication in this area arises from the impact of the CCD. The European Parliament wished to introduce a provision with a similar effect to section 75, but did so in a slightly different way. Because of the similarity between the two provisions, the approach adopted by the UK on implementation of the CCD was to retain section 75 as it was, but to introduce section 75A in order to cover cases which would fall within the CCD provision but not within section 75.

Accordingly, section 75A only applies to claims involving a cash price in excess of £30,000. Furthermore, in line with the general CCD scope, section 75A does not apply to agreements for business purposes or where the amount of credit exceeds £60,260. This approach can cause confusion, because it means the lower end of the scope is fixed by reference to the cash price of the vehicle, but the upper end is fixed by reference to the amount of credit provided.

Within these parameters, section 75A provides that a Customer under a 'linked credit agreement' may bring a claim against the Finance Company if they have a claim for breach of contract (though not misrepresentation) and either:

- The Seller cannot be traced, or has failed to respond to contact from the Customer; or

- The Customer has otherwise taken reasonable steps to pursue a claim against the Seller (not necessarily including litigation), but has been unable to 'obtain satisfaction' in the form of a replacement vehicle or compensation.

As a final point, it is worth highlighting that whilst s75A does not apply to business purpose contracts or those where the credit exceeds £60,260, both sections 56 and 75 do so.

CHAPTER TWELVE
POST-CONTRACT INFORMATION

In general law, once a motor vehicle finance agreement has been entered into, a Customer has no right to receive ongoing information about the state of their account, save in so far as such a right may have been specifically provided for in the contract itself. Of course, most Finance Companies will provide such information on request; this may be free of charge, as a matter of customer service, or may involve some payment by the Customer towards the administrative expense involved. In addition, Finance Companies will proactively provide relevant information if the Customer defaults on the payments due and the Finance Company is looking to get these arrears brought up to date, and would almost certainly expect to charge for doing so.

In the event of a breach, a Finance Company may decide that it wants to exercise its contractual right to end the agreement, recover and sell the vehicle to reduce the balance due, and pursue immediate payment of any shortfall from the Customer and/or a guarantor. Contrary to popular misconception, Finance Companies seldom do this without making genuine attempts to get the Customer to bring their account up to date. Apart from any other considerations, the early termination of a finance agreement, whether on default or settlement, can have a negative impact in accounting terms. In addition, motor vehicles are usually an essential item for both business and consumer Customers when it comes to earning money, including the money to pay the Finance Company. It is for this reason that motor vehicle instalments are generally regarded as being priority payments for budgeting purposes. As such, it is usually in the interests of the Finance Company to keep the Customer in the vehicle; if they don't, the Customer will almost certainly need to pay for an alternative, and payment of any shortfall due to the Finance Company will not be a priority.

This doesn't mean Finance Companies will not terminate if on balance they think it is in their interest to do so in order to minimise their loss. In this regard, the effect on the likely resale value of the vehicle is probably the major concern. This isn't just a question of continuing depreciation; it's also the fact that a Customer struggling to pay instalments is likely to skimp on other relevant costs, such as servicing and even insurance. Generally, though, Finance Companies will always look to provide Customers with information regarding their default and the potential consequences if it is not remedied.

That said, in general law it is very much up to each Finance Company as to exactly what information it provides to a defaulting Customer, and when. Furthermore, a Finance Company will invariably have the contractual power to terminate the agreement and recover the vehicle without any prior warning. Doing so in a simple arrears case would be highly unusual; in practice, there would almost always be some other factor involved, such as a perceived risk to the recovery of the vehicle if prior warning is given. However, even if not on a daily basis, such powers are regularly exercised by Finance Companies in respect of unregulated business agreements.

In the context of unregulated motor vehicle finance, therefore, Finance Companies are relatively free to provide post-contract information to, and pursue their contractual rights against, Customers much as they see fit The situation is, of course, entirely different in respect of consumers, who have certain rights in respect of the provision of information, and these rights effectively spill over into the business context in the form of regulated business purpose agreements. These rights are fairly limited in respect of hire agreements, but are much more extensive in relation to credit.

As originally introduced, the provisions for post-contract information in the 1974 Act were limited as regards any type of agreement for the finance of motor vehicles. Section 77 (not, as we shall see, to be confused with section 77A) gives the Customer a limited right to obtain a copy of a credit agreement, together with a statement providing certain information regarding the account; section 78 gives hirers a similar right. However, these provisions are limited in scope, not least because they require a request for information to be made by the Customer. If the Finance Company fails to comply with these sections, the agreement is unenforceable unless/until the Finance Company complies. However, it was for some time widely felt that the benefit to Customers provided by these sections was rather limited.

The situation regarding hire agreements is unchanged. This is part of a general trend in CCA regulation which means that the protections afforded to hirers are often more restricted than those provided to Customers purchasing vehicles on credit. This is partly an accident of history; when the 1974 Act was created, the vast majority of retail hire agreements were either short-term rentals, or related to low-value objects such as televisions and white goods. The long-term hire of more substantial objects such as motor vehicles by consumers was almost unheard of, so the focus of the 1974 Act was on credit based structures such as hire purchase and conditional sale. Those structures remain particularly important for motor vehicle finance, but the growth in recent years of long-term hire contracts for consumers means that a gap in protection has opened up. There does not appear to be any good reason in regulatory terms why the rights and protections afforded to a Customer should be so different for a 3 year personal contract hire agreement than a 3 year personal contract purchase. In each case the Customer is taking on similar obligations, both as regards the vehicle and their own financial commitment. However, given the FCA's clear reluctance to meddle too much in the fundamentals of consumer credit law, it is unlikely that much will be done in the near future to address this disparity.

Be that as it may, it remains the case at present that further rights have been introduced in respect of credit-based finance arrangements relating to the provision of post-contract information, and the first provision to mention was introduced as part of the implementation of the CCD; namely, section 77B of the 1974 Act.

Section 77B has no application to business purpose agreements, nor to those for the provision of credit exceeding £60,260. Where it does apply, though, a Finance Company must, on receiving a request from the Customer, provide a statement in the form of a table showing:

- The amount and number of future instalments; and
- A breakdown of how much of each instalment represents capital, and how much interest and charges.

Given their ability to obtain more useful settlement information by other means, this provision is again of limited assistance to Customers, and does require a request to be made. Of much wider application, though, is section 77A of the 1974 Act which provides that regular statements must be given in respect of fixed sum credit agreements.

The provision of regular statements for running account agreements, such as credit card arrangements and overdrafts, has been a feature of the 1974 Act since inception. However, no similar provision was felt necessary at the time in respect of fixed sum agreements until section 77A came into effect as part of the 2006 Act upgrade of CCA legislation. Statements provided under section 77A are often referred to as 'annual' statements. Strictly, section 77A statements have no particular fixed length, but as they must be provided at least once a year, for fairly obvious commercial reasons Finance Companies only tend to send them out annually; hence the form of common reference.

The provisions applying to the timing and content of annual statements are complex and not always easily comprehensible. Essentially, though, the regime works at follows:

- The Finance Company is required to give the Customer statements relating to a sequence of periods, commencing on the date that the agreement is made (or the date on which the credit is given, if later). This requirement continues until there is no longer any sum payable under the agreement.
- The Finance Company then has thirty days from the end of each period in which to send the statement out to the Customer.

It should be noted that these requirements have two practical effects. Firstly, there is no requirement for a section 77A statement to be given if the finance agreement is in fact fully paid up within the initial twelve month and thirty-day period. Conversely, though, it does mean that even an agreement which is intended to run for less than a year will require an annual statement to be given, if it is not in fact fully repaid within the one year and thirty-day period.

Assuming that the requirement for service is triggered, the Finance Company will need to ensure that the annual statement it sends out complies with the relevant regulations, which require specific information about the particular account to be given, along with some generic statutory wording. In many ways, an annual statement is very similar to a credit card statement. In addition to giving details of the relevant finance agreement, including the original amount of credit and the rate of interest applicable, the main body of the annual statement consists of an opening balance, details of the various movements on the account in the relevant period, and a closing balance. However, because of the different nature of regulated motor vehicle finance agreements, the 'movements on the account' which need to be detailed are somewhat different from a credit card agreement.

Regulated motor vehicle finance agreements present Customers with a fixed total payable which incorporates pre-calculated interest and charges. Since the opening balance on the first statement therefore already includes the charges for credit, it would clearly be confusing for the Finance Company to be required to display those charges as they actually fall due over the life of the agreement; accordingly, that is not required. For similar reasons, there is no requirement for the Finance Company to show instalments falling due. Essentially, therefore, an annual statement is effectively required to show payments received from the Customer, together with any additional charges that might have accrued (such as default charges). Some Finance Companies do feel that it helps Customers if they show instalments falling due, but such entries are for information only and do not have any effect on the running balance of the account.

In addition to these financial details, certain generic information must be given in each annual statement; in particular, a warning about the consequences of failure to pay on time, along with reminders about the Customers rights in respect of early settlement, complaints and (for HP and conditional sale) early termination.

Given the perceived importance of all this information, it was felt appropriate at the time that annual statements were introduced to provide that the consequences of a failure to supply them should be particularly punitive. These consequences do not apply only to a failure to send a statement at all. If a Finance Company fails to send an annual statement which complies strictly with all of the complex requirements of the relevant regulations, not only does the agreement become unenforceable until the Finance Company does send a statement in the correct form, but the Finance Company is also not entitled to charge any interest or default charges in respect of the period of non-compliance. In practice, this means that the remediation of any breaches of the requirements for annual statements involves the stripping out of any pre-calculated interest, so that it can be repaid and/or credited to the Customer (depending, of course, on whether it has in fact been paid).

The strictness of these provisions is slightly tempered by regulation 41 of the relevant regulations (often referred to as Reg 41), in that failures to comply which do not affect the substance of the required information can be disregarded. Nevertheless, since the introduction of section 77A, many Finance Companies have had to pay large sums of money to Customers by way of 'compensation' for minor breaches that have actually caused no detriment whatsoever.

Accordingly, whilst the thinking behind section 77A was clearly beneficial to Customers, it is less certain that it has always had a positive impact in practice. Windfall payments to Customers for minor breaches may sound all very well, but as with all consumer protection law, it is the Customer that has to pay the price in the long run in the form of higher finance charges.

The other major information provision introduced by the 2006 Act, which is in some ways similar to section 77A, is the requirement under section 86B for a Finance Company to give a Customer a Notice of Sums in Arrears (NOSIA).

In the wider sense of the word, a Customer will be in 'arrears' as and when any sum is overdue for payment under the terms of the relevant agreement. Finance Companies, like other creditors, have always taken steps to inform Customers when this occurs, and to seek repayment. However, it was felt that decisions about the quantity and quality of such information should not be left up to the Finance Company involved; furthermore, that such information needed to be accompanied by specific warnings to the Customer, and pointers as to where to obtain assistance.

NOSIAs apply in different ways to running account agreements, but for the purposes of motor vehicle finance, the requirements are set out in section 86B of the 1974 Act and detailed regulations. The same regulations also govern the requirements for section 77A and are equally obscure and difficult to interpret when it comes to section 86B. Also as with section 77A, the effects of failure to comply strictly with these regulations are similarly punitive; the agreement is not only unenforceable, but the Finance Company is not entitled to charge interest and/or default charges during the relevant period of breach. It is worth repeating that the interest in question is not limited to 'default' interest, but extends to cover the interest which forms part of the standard charges. On the other hand, unlike section 77A, section 86B also applies to regulated hire agreements, though the effects of non-compliance are to some extent reduced by the fact that hire rentals do not technically incorporate any element of interest.

Although the technicalities are difficult to apply, the broad intentions of the NOSIA regime are fairly straightforward. Clearly, there needs to be a statutory definition of arrears to act as a trigger for service of the relevant notice, and for these purposes the bar is set at a sum equivalent to the last two regular payments falling due under the agreement. These payments may be rentals or instalments, depending on the nature of the agreement, but for the purposes of setting this bar, it is only the regular payments that count; ad hoc payments, such as default charges do not. On the other hand, all overdue payments under the agreement, including default charges, are taken into account when calculating the amount of the arrears. The maths is then simple; if the amount of the arrears exceeds the sum of the last two regular payments, then the Finance Company must serve a NOSIA within fourteen days.

Service of NOSIAs has two distinct stages. When the Customer first enters the state of being in statutory arrears, a first NOSIA needs to be served. In essence, this notice informs the Customer that they are 'in arrears' and provides details of the relevant sums, but does little more in financial terms. Most of the content of a first NOSIA is taken up with the provision of statutory information, including the FCA required sheet on how to deal with arrears. Once a Customer has entered this position of being 'in arrears', they effectively stay in that position unless and until either the Finance Company obtains a court judgment or there are no longer any sums overdue for payment under the agreement. It is important to note that in this context it is not the original arrears that matter; if any sum whatsoever is overdue, then the arrears position continues.

It is during this continued arrears position that second NOSIAs are required, at six-monthly intervals. A second or 'subsequent' NOSIA is very different from a first NOSIA. Certain statutory information needs to be given, but the core of a subsequent NOSIA is a mini statement detailing the state of the Customer's account since the issue of the previous NOSIA (which may be either a first NOSIA or a subsequent NOSIA, depending on how long the Customer remains 'in arrears').

In the same way as for a section 77A statement, a subsequent NOSIA needs to state the opening and closing balances on the account, together with any movements which lead from one to the other. In addition, though, the Finance Company needs to keep the Customer informed about the state of their arrears, by also providing details of the opening and closing balances for this part of the overall sum due.

As with section 77A statements, the requirements for service of NOSIAs in the right form and at the right time have proved difficult for Finance Companies, and the consequences of failure to comply are particularly rigid. Furthermore, where a Customer is in arrears, a breach of either section 77A or section 86B can lead to cross-contamination. Because the need to conduct a remediation exercise in respect of either will have a retrospective effect on the state of the account, it automatically follows that the information given in the other type of notice must also have been incorrect and require remediation. This can make such remediation exercises particularly complex to put into effect.

Another element of post-contractual information that was felt to be deficient in the run up to the CCA 2006 related to the imposition of default charges. These charges, of which letter charges are the most commonplace, are sums of money payable by the Customer if the agreement is breached. As such, they represent a form of liquidated damages clause and are subject to the usual rules on penalties and fairness. The particular problem identified by Regulators, however, was the fact that in many cases Customers were not even aware that such charges were being added to their account. As a result, provision was introduced to require Finance Companies to give Customers formal notification in the form of a Notice of Default Sums.

If a Finance Company adds a default sum to a Customer's account, notice must be sent within thirty five days. This extended period is intended to allow for the service of combined notices of default sums where more than one default notice is added to an account at around the same time. Essentially, Finance Companies are entitled to sweep up all default charges on a monthly basis, and give a single notice setting out details.

It was also felt to be wrong that Finance Companies were able to charge interest on default sums unless and until the Customer had been given an opportunity to pay them. Many Finance Companies do not, in fact, charge such interest, but some do. In any event, Finance Companies are now prevented from charging default interest on default sums unless that sum is still outstanding twenty nine days after the service of the relevant notice.

CHAPTER THIRTEEN EARLY SETTLEMENT

Once again, in general law the right of a Customer to settle a motor vehicle finance agreement early is entirely governed by the terms of the agreement itself. As indicated elsewhere, allowing an agreement to be ended early can have negative consequences for a Finance Company. However, in this context, it is possible for an agreement term allowing early settlement to pass the effect of those consequences on to the Customer, by requiring them to be taken into account when calculating the required settlement figure.

It is normal practice even for unregulated business motor vehicle finance credit agreements to incorporate pre-calculated charges, because doing so provides the Customer with certainty up front regarding the regular instalments that will need to be made. This process obviously involves calculating the interest that would fall due throughout the finance period and adding it to the credit advanced in order to work out the total that will be paid and the required instalments. This means that if the Customer were to repay early, it could be unfair for them to have to pay the full balance outstanding, because it would almost certainly include some element of anticipated interest relating to the period after the date of settlement. On the other hand, since the Finance Company's charges are spread out across the hire term, some of this anticipated interest will relate to the Finance Company's anticipated profit and administration costs which have already incurred.

In theory, there is no reason why an unregulated business credit agreement could not require payment of the full balance; such elements of the unfair contract terms law as apply to business contracts are concerned with regulating clauses which seek to allow a party to avoid or limit their performance of the contract terms, which would not be the case here. Nevertheless, it is not unusual for even unregulated business credit agreements to give the Customer a right to settle early, and to provide for some rebate to be given if they do so. In general, such provisions are drafted to ensure that the Finance Company will not lose out, after taking into account its anticipated profit and expenses to date, as well as any further costs it will incur on settlement. Those costs will undoubtedly cover the additional administration involved, but will typically also extend to what are commonly referred to as 'break costs'; in other words, any costs which the Finance Company might have to pay in order to adjust its own borrowing arrangements in the wholesale finance market so as to accommodate the Customer's desire for early settlement.

Similar considerations apply to unregulated business motor vehicle hire agreements. As with credit based structures, the Finance Company will almost certainly have only purchased the vehicle for the purpose of entering into the specific contract, and is entitled to take the view that it will not agree to the early return of that vehicle unless it receives a payment which ensures that it will not lose out by doing so. Many commercial hire arrangements do not even contain a provision for early return, though in practice most Finance Companies will allow this to happen; they just deal with the payment issue if and when the Customer makes a request for early return.

As for credit based structures, payment of the full outstanding rentals would be unfair to the Customer, so a rebate is usually given. How this rebate is calculated is up to the Finance company, which will take into account additional administrative expense and its own break costs. In practice, though, there are two commonplace approaches, depending on the nature of the hire agreement.

For finance leases, where it is always intended that the Customer will get the benefit of the sale proceeds of the vehicle, the full balance of future rentals will normally become due, with the Customer receiving credit for the net proceeds of the sale of the vehicle and a rebate that is usually somewhere in the region of 3% to 5% of the value of future rentals. For operating leases, where it is not intended that the Customer will get the benefit of the sale proceeds of the vehicle, the Customer will only be required to return the vehicle in the right condition (or pay any charges that may be required to put it into such condition) and to pay something in the region of 50% of the future rentals.

This, then, is the general position, but as ever there are additional protections for Customers in respect of regulated agreements built into the 1974 Act. Before looking at these in detail, it is worthwhile noting that they have no application to hire agreements. As will be seen, the Customer under a regulated credit agreement has the right to end it early, repay the sums that are due, and receive the benefit of a rebate. However, no similar protection was thought to be necessary in respect of hire agreements at the time the 1974 Act was drafted; nor has there been any subsequent move to introduce equivalent provisions. As such, Customers under a regulated motor vehicle hire agreements generally have no right to end it early.

There is a limited right in section 101 of the 1974 Act to end hire agreements early, but this is in practice aimed at long-running and low-value consumer items such as televisions. Section 101 provides that at any time after eighteen months of hire, the Customer can give notice bringing the agreement to an end and cease to make further payments. The section does not, however, apply to a business purpose agreement, nor to any hire agreement where the total annual rentals exceed £1,500. Accordingly, whilst section 101 could in theory apply to a motor vehicle finance agreement, it would in practice be exceedingly rare for it to do so.

Accordingly, the early termination of a regulated motor vehicle hire agreement is again dependent entirely on the terms of the contract itself. Where any right to settlement is given to a consumer, the legislation relating to unfair terms in consumer contracts (of which more elsewhere) would require this provision to operate in a fair and balanced manner, and this would be the case whether the agreement were regulated or unregulated. Broadly, though, the two approaches to settlement payments for unregulated agreements outlined above are seen as being fair, provide that they can be shown to do no more than compensate the Finance Company.

Returning then to credit, the Customer as indicated always has an unconditional right to bring a regulated credit agreement to an end early by making payment in full, and in doing so to receive a rebate of the finance charges. This right has since been extended by the CCD reforms to apply as well to partial settlements. As such, any payment (whether or not made by the Customer themselves) which effectively repays an element of the finance provided under a regulated agreement before the date on which it was due to be paid, will attract a rebate.

Strictly, there is no requirement for a Finance Company to adopt the statutory basis for calculating this rebate. It can, if it wishes, adopt an alternative (and potentially even more generous) basis if it wishes to do so, provided that it can be shown to be no less generous than the statutory minimum. However, for obvious practical and commercial reasons, it would be unusual for a Finance Company not to adopt the statutory formula.

Essentially, the 1974 Act settlement provisions are designed to strike a balance between the interests of the Customer and those of the Finance Company, but in a manner that is less geared to ensuring that the Finance Company recovers all profit and expense. Accordingly, the broad principle underlying the provisions set out in sections 94 and 95 of the 1974 Act, and in the settlement regulations, is that the Customer should only be responsible for those elements of the agreed finance charges as relate to the period prior to the date on which the agreement is settled. The detailed settlement regulations are therefore intended to ensure that the Customer receives a rebate in respect of such charges as relate to the period after that date, albeit adjusted slightly to provide the Finance Company with a margin to reflect their anticipated profit and additional administrative expense. The Finance Company is entitled to make a further adjustment in respect of break costs in accordance with section 95A, but the conditions for doing so mean that this is unusual in the context of motor vehicle finance.

It is important to remember that these provisions are not limited to circumstances in which the Customer is making a voluntary payment. Since a rebate needs to be given whenever any element of a Customer's indebtedness is effectively repaid early, the regulations also apply in less obvious circumstances, such as where an agreement is terminated early by the Finance Company. The terms of the agreement may provide for a full rebate to be given at that point, in which case no further rebate would be due. However, whilst this is common practice, it is not strictly necessary unless the termination involves an early payment (for example, where the vehicle has been written off and an insurance payment made). Accordingly, if they don't adopt such a practice, it is important for the Finance Company to remember that payments received post termination may require a rebate to be given to the Customer (for example, on receipt of the vehicle sale proceeds). The only real exception to the rebate requirement is when a Customer has exercised their section 99 option to VT an HP or conditional sale agreement; in that limited situation, the Customer's liability is controlled by section 100, and sections 94 and 95 have no application.

All that said, one of the most common circumstances in which a rebate is required in the context of motor vehicle finance is when a Customer wishes to trade in a vehicle before the end of the finance term, as part of arrangements to obtain a new vehicle. It will often be a motor dealer who will make contact with the Finance Company to request settlement information. However, when this happens, the Dealer is strictly doing so on behalf of the Customer, so the Finance Company will always need to act as if the request came direct from the Customer, and comply with the settlement provisions accordingly.

Whether it is the Customer or the Dealer that does so, even a verbal request for settlement information will act as a formal notification of the Customer's wish to settle early. Giving such notice does not bind the Customer to settle, but does require the Finance Company to provide certain information in order that the Customer may decide if they wish to do so. Detailed regulations govern both the form of the settlement statement and the calculation of the information which it contains; in particular, the way in which the 'settlement date' is fixed and the rebate of charges which is to be provided.

Customers are often less than happy with the amount of rebate that they will be given, particularly in the latter stages of a finance term. This is usually because the Customer has assumed that charges accrue equally across the period of finance, so that each repayment is made up of the same proportions of capital and charge, but this is not the case. The Finance Company deliberately structures the payments on a flat basis because this makes it easier for the Customer to budget for regular payments, but the charges strictly accrue against a reducing capital balance, which means that payments towards the beginning of the finance term contain a higher proportion of charges than those at the end. This is why section 77B (see above) requires the Customer to be provided on request with information which makes the actual repayment of capital and interest over the period of finance clear.

When a Customer enters into a regulated agreement, the Finance Company is required to calculate the relevant APR by reference to the actual timing of the credits, charges and repayments that should occur throughout the term of the agreement. Essentially, the prescribed methodology for dealing with early settlement is the reverse of the APR process, with the Finance Company being required to work out how much of the charges actually relate to the period after the point of settlement date. As for APR calculation, this requires the application of a complicated actuarial formula.

Before this formula can be applied, however, the Finance Company needs to identify the 'settlement date', To ensure a standard approach by Finance Companies, the settlement regulations provide that this will be either the twenty-eighth day after the Customer's request is received, or any later date specified by the Customer in that request. Once it knows the settlement date, the Finance Company can then work out the rebate that will be due in respect of subsequent finance charges.

However, although that rebate is calculated by reference to the prescribed settlement date, it is not necessarily the rebate as of that date. The method of calculation set out in the settlement regulations does allow a Finance Company, if the original agreement was for a period of more than one year, to defer the settlement date for the purposes of that calculation by a month or thirty days. It is important to remember that doing so does not defer the actual settlement date; that remains unchanged. What it effectively does is to allow the Finance Company to exclude from the rebate (and thereby retain) the charges that would have accrued during the deferral period. Either way, once the rebate has been calculated, the Finance Company simply works out the required settlement figure by taking the balance that would be due on the settlement date (assuming that any intermediate payments are made) and deducting the statutory rebate.

Once that settlement figure has been calculated, the Finance Company will provide the Customer with a settlement statement in the form required by the settlement regulations, and in practice will also inform any dealer involved. If that settlement figure is paid on or before the specified settlement date, then the agreement will end and title in the vehicle will transfer to the Customer. On the other hand, if the Customer does not pay by the settlement date, then a further settlement figure will need to be calculated, as at a subsequent settlement date, incorporating an amended rebate.

As an aside, it is important to remember that in these cases, whilst the money paid to the Finance Company will come from the dealer rather than from the Customer direct, the payment is nevertheless made on behalf of the Customer. As such, the payment made discharges the Customer's obligations under the finance agreement and leads to a transfer of title in the vehicle to the Customer, which the Customer then passes on to the dealer under the trade in arrangements. The fact that payment may be made by the dealer does not mean that the dealer is agreeing to purchase the vehicle from the Finance Company. Accordingly, the Finance Company's obligations in respect of the vehicle, particularly as regards its condition, are still defined only by the finance agreement.

Turning then to partial voluntary settlement by a Customer, the relevant provisions are in some ways similar to those which apply in respect of full settlement, but there are important differences. For a start, there is no prescribed process to allow a Customer to obtain advance information from the Finance Company about the potential rebate. The Customer does have a right to obtain a statement confirming the rebate applied, and the effect of the part payment on their subsequent payment obligations, but this right only arises once the part payment has actually been made.

In the circumstances, the Customer has a simple right to notify the Finance Company that they intend to repay part of their debt early. This notice fixes the 'settlement date' in the same way as for full settlement, and a rebate will be due to the Customer if the intended part payment is made within the 28 day settlement period. Again, this notice does not need to be in writing. In practice, it doesn't even need to be verbal, in that simply overpaying under the agreement will amount to the giving of such a notice. In any event, once it has been 'notified', it is up to the Finance Company to work out the relevant rebate to be applied to the account with effect from the 'settlement date', which it again does in much the same way as for full settlement, with one obvious difference; instead of applying the rebate formula to all future charges, it effectively applies it only to that proportion of those charges which relate to the capital which is being repaid early by the Customer.

Once the rebate has been calculated, the Customer will receive credit against the balance outstanding under the agreement on the 'settlement date', which again may not be the same as the date on which the settlement payment is made. Either way, though, it will be appreciated that partial settlement will inevitable reduce the amount remaining payable under the agreement, which will need to be reflected in an adjustment to the subsequent payment structure. In simplistic terms, either the amount of the future payments can remain unchanged, in which case fewer payments will be needed in order to discharge the full balance under the agreement, or the number of future payments can remain the same, in which case the amount of each will need to be reduced. Strictly, which option is adopted is up to the Finance Company, not the Customer. As indicated above, the Customer has a right to know what the effect will be, but they cannot tell the Finance Company which option it should choose.

Lastly, as mentioned above, there are circumstances other than voluntary early settlement in which a full or partial rebate may be required to be given to a Customer; in addition, if a Default Notice (or and similar statutory notice) requires an accelerated payment to be made by the Customer, information must be given regarding the rebate that would be due if that payment is made. In the latter case, the 'settlement date' will be the date specified for the expiry of the relevant notice; in any other case it will be the date on which the relevant payment was received by the Finance Company. In any event, the process for calculating the rebate will be the same as for a voluntary settlement; either full or partial, depending on the circumstances.

CHAPTER FOURTEEN
EARLY TERMINATION BY THE CUSTOMER

In some ways similar to early settlement, the right of a Customer in general law to terminate their credit agreement and return the vehicle to a Finance Company is entirely dependent on the contract terms. For obvious reasons, no such right will attach to a loan; the Customer, as the owner of the vehicle, will be free to sell it and use the proceeds towards payment of the loan balance, but that is a different point altogether. It is unusual for Finance Companies to give the Customer a contractual right to terminate early and return the vehicle; as indicated elsewhere, such arrangements can involve loss for the Finance Company. That said, it is not unheard of for Finance Companies to allow a Customer to do this, provided they pay any shortfall on the agreement balance after the vehicle has been sold, together with any break costs and administration expenses incurred by the Finance Company.

As with other general law situations, though, this position was seen as creating particular detriment for consumers and the 1974 Act incorporates a special right of early termination applicable to some regulated credit agreements. Voluntary Termination under section 99, often just referred to as 'VT', is the right for a Customer to bring an HP or conditional sale agreement to an end early. Such early termination does not involve full payment; rather, it is a means by which the Customer can return the vehicle to the Finance Company and restrict their liability in respect of the balance remaining due. The calculation of this residual liability under section 100 is often referred to as the 'one half rule', because it is made by reference to one half of the total payable under the agreement.

The first thing to remember about sections 99 and 100 is that the Customer's right to VT is wholly unfettered. It is still sometimes mistakenly thought that the Customer needs to have paid one half of the total payable under the agreement before they are able to exercise the right, but this is incorrect; a Customer can VT at any time. Strictly, in order to do so, the Customer should give written notification to the Finance Company. However, if the Customer gives any sort of unequivocal indication that they wish to avail themselves of the benefits of a VT, the Finance Company would normally have little option but to comply, regardless of the technical requirements for notice.

A Finance Company will often try to discuss the matter with a Customer, on the basis that if there is a genuine financial issue, it may be possible for it to be addressed without the need for the vehicle to be returned and the agreement unwound. If, though, the Customer is set on exercising the option, then the Finance Company will need to make arrangements to recover the vehicle and to calculate any further payment that may be due from the Customer. This latter point can cause confusion.

Under section 100, the Customer remains liable to pay any sums, including arrears, that have already fallen due under the agreement; in addition, the Customer is liable to pay any shortfall between the aggregate of sums paid and due, and one half of the total payable under the agreement. If the Customer's payments and the amount of any arrears already exceed one half of the total payable (which is, of course, calculated as including any deposit or advance payment made), then nothing further will be due, provided the vehicle is in the right condition.

As regards the vehicle, that is to be returned to the Finance Company, which is entitled to sell it and retain the net proceeds in full; the Customer gets no benefit from the sale. The Customer is, though, required to have looked after the vehicle in accordance with the agreement terms whilst it was in their possession, and will have to compensate the Finance Company if they have not done so and the value of the vehicle has suffered as a result. This will, as for the return of contract hire vehicles, be something to be assessed on a case by case basis, generally using accepted industry standards for 'fair wear and tear'.

The provision is intended to be a rough rule of thumb, under which Customers can escape full liability if their financial circumstances deteriorate. When first introduced, the provision was intended to strike a reasonable balance between the interests of the Customer and the Finance Company. Unfortunately, Finance Companies tend to lose more in respect of the VTs than originally anticipated. This is, perhaps, just a fact of life as regards Customers who are in genuine financial difficulty. However, it would appear that a large proportion of VT's are not the result of financial difficulties on the part of the Customer, but are instigated by dealers as a cheaper way of getting the Customer out of the existing vehicle and into a new one than would be the case if a full settlement were paid, As such, the right to VT, whilst being in some ways an important consumer protection, is also a cost of finance which is ultimately paid by all Customers as part of their finance charges.

CHAPTER FIFTEEN
EARLY TERMINATION BY THE FINANCE COMPANY

Whilst all parties to a finance agreement like to believe that no problems will occur, and that all payments will be made in full and on time, some level of collections and recovery activity by Finance Companies is bound to be necessary. Even over recent years, when default levels have consistently been at record lows, the need to take steps to enforce payment has still remained.

In general law, the legal aspects of such activity are relatively simple. There are, as already mentioned, general rules which restrict overly aggressive, or otherwise misleading, activities by traders, which extend to collection tactics. However, whilst such behaviour is not unknown within the motor vehicle finance industry, it is relatively rare compared to the vast number of vehicle finance contracts that are entered into year on year.

The approach of a Finance Company looking to enforce an unregulated agreement can be fairly simplistic. If Customers don't pay, then steps will be taken to chase arrears, and if the finance agreement cannot be brought back into line fairly quickly, this will undoubtedly result in the termination of the finance agreement. This will in turn lead to the Finance Company taking active steps to both repossess its vehicle and pursue payment of the outstanding shortfall.

In general terms, a Finance Company's right to terminate an agreement depends on the terms of the contract itself. It is normal for small breaches of any contract to be overlooked; indeed, it would not be acceptable for minor breaches to be used as grounds for terminating a consumer contract. On the other hand, finance agreements inevitably contain clauses providing that in certain circumstances, the Finance Company will be able to bring the relationship to an end.

These circumstances usually involve some form of default on the part of the Customer, though this isn't always necessary. An example of the latter would be where an agreement has been terminated because the vehicle has been destroyed, and an insurance payout has effectively settled most, if not all of the balance outstanding. In such a case, the agreement still needs technically to be brought to an end, so that the hiring of the vehicle is formally ended, and any remaining balance due is paid by the Customer.

More often, early termination is the result of a breach on the part of the Customer; usually, a breach as regards payment. In contract law, failure to pay is not necessarily a fundamental breach, entitling the other party to terminate. However, the need to receive payments on time and to process them with the minimum of administration is so central to a finance contract that such agreements invariably contain a 'hell or high water' clause, requiring the Customer to pay in full and on time, come what may. By making failure to pay a fundamental breach, the Finance Company ensures that it will be able to exercise a termination clause entitling it to bring the whole arrangement to an end. It doesn't have to do so immediately, but has the freedom to do so if it considers it necessary.

Although it is the failure to pay that most often leads to the default termination of a motor vehicle finance agreement, the main consideration for the Finance Company is usually the vehicle. It is commonplace for a Finance Company to talk of its 'security' in the vehicle. This is not 'security' in the technical legal sense. Formal 'security', such as the provision of a third-party guarantee or a charge on other property, is always possible, but not necessary. However, the vehicle itself is a valuable asset, which in the vast majority of finance arrangements will be owned by the Finance Company at the point of Customer default. Recovery and sale of this asset is likely to considerably reduce the amount owing to the Finance Company; hence the habit of regarding hire, HP and conditional sale agreements as not being wholly unsecured in the way loans are.

This viewpoint has two effects if a Customer is in default. One the one hand, it provides the Finance Company with an element of reassurance that at least a substantial part of its exposure to the Customer is likely to be recovered. On the other hand, leaving the vehicle with the Customer will reduce the potential value on resale, through a combination of additional use, general depreciation and the fact that Customers in financial difficulties tend to skimp on non-essential spending such as servicing and comprehensive insurance cover.

As a result, Finance Companies need to judge carefully whether, and if so when, to exercise their right to terminate. This will involve consideration of the Customer's interests as well as its own. A motor vehicle is often an essential asset for both businesses and consumers, and loss of use can have serious consequences. On the other hand, it is not necessarily in the Customer's interests for them to be allowed to keep the vehicle short term, if doing so increases their longer term liability. In any event, a Finance Company's overriding desire is always to get the agreement back on track as quickly and cheaply as it can, if that is going to be possible. Repossession is always a last resort, to be exercised only if and when the Finance Company balance are which the vehicle.

This is the underlying position for all motor vehicle Finance Companies, even those which are not authorised by the FCA. For those that are authorised, though, particularly those which engage in regulated consumer finance, the balance to be struck is subtly different. The underlying principles of FCA regulation, including of course TCF, apply to any authorised entity; how those principles apply may vary between business and consumer activity, but they still apply to both. Furthermore, if the agreement is regulated, the 'forbearance' requirements set out the consumer credit section of the FCA's Handbook (CONC) will apply, albeit again with variations between business and consumer activity. Overall, the same balance needs to be struck, but things are slightly shifted in favour of the Customer. The Finance Company cannot always put its own interests first, but needs to be able to show that it has paid due regard to those of the Customer.

This doesn't necessarily make for a substantially different approach to termination by authorised Finance Companies. It is true that a consumer agreement is generally only regarded as being in 'default' once it is at least two payments down, whereas business agreements are usually treated as being so after one missed payment. However, the need to balance the benefits of leaving the vehicle in the Customer's possession against those of repossession is fundamentally unchanged.

Assuming the Finance Company does decide to terminate the finance arrangement, this will involve dealing with two elements. Firstly, for reasons explained elsewhere, the Finance Company will wish to bring to an end the Customer's right to possession and use of the vehicle, so that it can be recovered and sold. Secondly, the Finance Company will wish to ensure that the Customer is required to make such payment as may be necessary in order to ensure that it does not end up out of pocket once.

The first element is relatively straightforward. Once the agreement has been terminated, the Customer's right to possession and use of the vehicle will automatically end, and the Finance Company will once more be entitled to immediate possession of its asset. Failure by the Customer to return the vehicle at this stage would now amount to a wrongful interference with the Finance Company's rights of ownership, and a court order for delivery up could normally be obtained if repossession agents are unable to recover it. As we will see, there are restrictions on the repossession of vehicles subject to regulated agreements which mean that such court orders are more often required in that segment of the market.

The second element will vary depending upon the nature of the relevant agreement. Longer term motor vehicle finance agreements are one off arrangements. The Finance Company buys the vehicle for the sole purpose of entering into the proposed contract. If the contract ends early because the Customer is in breach, the Finance Company is entitled to be put into the same position it would have been in had the contract been performed. In all cases, therefore, a Finance Company will start to assess its loss on the basis that it should be entitled to recover the payments it would have received from the Customer had the termination not been necessary.

These arrangements for a Finance Company to be paid the future balance are what lawyers refer to as 'liquidated damages' clauses. In other words, rather than being unascertained, the agreement itself defines the amount of compensation that needs to be paid in respect of the breach. Such clauses have the distinct advantage of avoiding the need in many cases for the level of damages to be ascertained by a court. However, even in commercial arrangements, the parties are not entirely free to agree the level of damages that will be payable. In order to operate successfully, a liquidated damages clause must amount to a genuine pre-estimate of the loss that is likely to be suffered by the Finance Company as a result of the breach. This estimate does not need to be absolutely accurate, but does need to be realistic. If it is not, then it will be struck out by a court as a 'penalty'; in other words, a punitive clause designed to overcompensate for the breach. In the circumstances, even a business purposes contract cannot go too far, and of course (as described elsewhere) any consumer contract would be subject to the unfair terms legislation.

Exactly how such clauses work in practice will depend on the underlying nature of the relevant agreement; in particular, whether it is hire or credit based, and whether or not it has a full pay out structure. In a full pay out agreement, such as a finance lease or HP, the payments due from the Customer represent the Finance Company's entire interest in the transaction, and for it to receive those payments and the sale proceeds of the vehicle would involve a windfall profit. As such, the termination provisions in such an agreement will be structured so that whilst the Finance Company is entitled to recover the balance of the future payments that it should have received under the agreement, credit will be given for the sale proceeds of the vehicle (net of the costs of repossession and sale) once it has been recovered and sold.

This sounds simple enough, but the balance of payments will also need to be adjusted. In the same way as for early settlement, there will at the point of termination often be some proportion of the balance due under a credit agreement which represents charges that have not yet accrued. Even in respect of a hire agreement, the balance of future rentals will need to be discounted in order to reflect the fact that they will (in theory at least) be received early; often referred to as 'accelerated receipt'. Accordingly, the relevant clauses will need to provide for these factors to be taken into account, and this would normally be done by providing that the Customer will receive a rebate, in respect of credit charges or a discount for accelerated receipt of rentals, as the case may be.

The timing for this rebate can vary. The rebate needs to reflect early receipt of funds, but in practice early payment will not often happen at the point of termination. As such, there is strictly nothing wrong with a termination clause that provides for the appropriate rebate to be given if and when funds are in fact received early. On the other hand, some Finance Companies find it much simpler to apply the necessary rebate at the point of termination. Doing so has administrative benefits, and can simplify the collections process. It does, of course, mean that the Customer is always given the maximum rebate available even though early payment has in most cases not yet been made. On the other hand, stripping out the rebate means that the Finance Company is entitled to exercise its right to charge default interest on the full amount of the reduced balance from the date of termination.

The situation is slightly more complicated when it comes to partial pay out finance structures, such as operating leases. The same principles apply, but a further adjustment is required to take account of the fact that the Finance Company always anticipated receiving part of the proceeds of sale of the vehicle in any event. It would therefore be unfair if the Finance Company were to be required to apply this residual value against the future payments due from the Customer. On the other hand, since the vehicle is being returned early, there is a real chance that it will be worth more than the residual value. In practice, therefore, whilst the Finance Company does not need to give credit for the entire sale proceeds of the vehicle, it does need to give credit for any excess above the residual value. As such, a valid liquidated damages clause will provide that the balance of rentals will be payable, subject to a discount for accelerated receipt and credit for this excess sale value (if and when received).

Matters such as termination and repossession inevitably become more complex when an agreement is regulated, and it has been deemed inappropriate for Finance Companies to pursue their own interests in a wholly unrestricted manner.

As seen elsewhere, many of the 1974 Act provisions are predicated on the concept that Customers should be given relevant information as a matter of course. In this context, however, the requirements go beyond simply informing Customers of the fact and consequences of any breach; the Finance Company will only be able to act on a breach if the required information has been given.

In particular, a specific form of notice needs to be given to the Customer if the Finance Company wishes to:

- terminate the agreement;
- repossess the vehicle;
- accelerate any payment due; or
- enforce any security.

It is important to remember that the giving of such notices is not limited to circumstances which involve a default by the Customer; neither are Default Notices required to give Customers an opportunity to remedy the default in all circumstances. That said, it is true to say that in practice by far the vast majority of notices served in these circumstances are Default Notices which give the Customer an opportunity to remedy; most usually, by paying the arrears that have accrued.

Of course, the Finance Company must be contractually entitled to do any of these things. However, assuming that it is, the Default Notice regime effectively provides that the Finance Company is not entitled to exercise those contractual rights unless and until it has given the Customer prior warning. There are a number of reasons for this. The first, and most obvious, is that if the default is capable of being remedied, it would be unfair for a consumer not to be given the opportunity to remedy it. The Customer therefore needs to be informed of the breach, what needs to be done to remedy it and by what date, and of the consequences if they do not do so.

A Default Notice therefore needs to set out sufficient information to allow the Customer to be certain about their position, and what they may need to do to avoid the specified consequences. It also needs to give certain statutory information, such as details of where the Customer may be able to find help to deal with the problem. The notice must also highlight the Customer's right to apply for a Time Order; indeed, contrary to popular belief, Customers are generally not able to apply for Time Orders at all until they have received a Default Notice, or one of the equivalent notices. Most importantly in the context of motor vehicle finance, the required information in respect of an HP or conditional sale agreement includes a reminder to Customers who have paid more than one third of the total payable that the vehicle is 'protected goods' for the purposes of section 90 of the 1974 Act.

Essentially, therefore, a Default Notice gives the Customer prior warning of the consequences of their breach of the agreement. In most cases, that breach may be remediable, but in others it will not. If it isn't, then a Default Notice will still need to be served, and the same time period given to the Customer before any action is taken. However, in such a case there will be no question of the Finance Company not taking the specified action; the Default Notice acts only as a warning, provides essential information, and activates the Customer's right to apply for a Time Order.

As regards timing, there is no specific trigger for the giving of a Default Notice; a Finance Company is able to pick and choose when it does so, depending on its own approach to collections activity. As indicated elsewhere, TCF and forbearance requirements under the FCA Handbook do place some limits on a Finance Company's right to regard a breach of an agreement as being sufficient to justify giving the Customer formal notification of 'default', particularly when the Customer is a consumer. However, whilst these requirements may act to prevent a Finance Company giving a Default Notice too quickly, they do not otherwise control when it must be given. All that the 1974 Act requires is that the Default Notice is given, and the relevant statutory period is allowed to expire, before the Finance Company takes any of the relevant contractual steps.

As far as a Default Notice is concerned, the relevant statutory period is fourteen days after the service of the notice. Default Notices are an exception to the general rule that CCA documentation can be served by electronic means. Accordingly, a Default Notice must either be handed personally to the Customer, or sent by first class pre-paid post. If posted, it will be deemed to be received on the second working day after it was sent. Allowing for the potential effect of bank holidays, this means the minimum standard period for compliance with a Default Notice is eighteen days after it is posted, but in practice most Finance Companies adopt a period of twenty one days.

As a final point on the giving of Default Notices (and most other CCA prescribed documentation), the 1974 Act states that a document is 'given' if it is posted. Strictly, therefore, a Finance Company complies with its obligations under section 87 when it posts a Default Notice to a Customer, and will be able to act freely after the statutory period has expired regardless of whether the notice is in fact received by the Customer.

As indicated above, there can be circumstances in which a Finance Company will wish to bring a finance agreement to an end, or take one or other of the restricted actions, without there having been any breach of the agreement by the Customer. Obviously, in such circumstances, service of a Default Notice would not be appropriate, since there has been no default. Accordingly, the 1974 Act provides alternative, but equivalent, mechanisms for the Finance Company to use. Section 76 provides that a Finance Company must serve a statutory notice before exercising a non-default contractual right to repossess a vehicle, accelerate any payment due, or enforce security; section 98 provides that similar notice must be given before the Finance Company can exercises a non-default right to terminate the agreement.

The relevant regulations governing such notices provide that Finance Companies are entitled to issue a combined section 76/98 form of notice, and doing so is general practice. Such forms of notice are sometimes confusingly referred to as 'Termination Notices'. However, all this really means is that they amount to notice of the Finance Company's intention to terminate; it does not mean that such a notice needs to be given as the precursor to the exercise of the right to terminate. Whether based on a default or non-default clause, there is no statutory format for the contractual termination of a regulated agreement. Doing so is a pure matter of contract law. It may be better, for the purposes of certainty, evidence and TCF, to ensure that termination is in writing, but if the contract allows it to be done by other means, then that will be effective.

A section 76/98 Notice needs to set out sufficient information to allow the Customer to be certain about their position, and to give certain statutory information, such as details of where the Customer may be able to find help to deal with the problem. The notice must also highlight the Customer's right to apply for a Time Order. As with a Default Notice, the relevant statutory period must be allowed to expire before the Finance Company takes any of the relevant contractual steps. However, the statutory period in respect of a section 76 /98 Notice is less than it is for a Default Notice. As originally enacted, the period was seven days for sections 76, 98 and 87. The period for a Default Notice was subsequently extended to fourteen days, but these arrangements do not apply to sections 76 or 98, so the standard period applied to such notices is only fourteen from posting, rather than twenty one days.

Having terminated its agreement, after of course serving the necessary prior warning notice if that agreement is regulated, a Finance Company will need to address the practicalities of repossession and collections. Dealing firstly with the question of repossession, Finance Companies will usually procure the services of specialist agents, who are experienced in dealing with both the technical issues involved, and the somewhat difficult conversations that the process inevitably involves. Likewise, whilst a Finance Company will normally engage in collections activity at a distance, it may also utilise the services of a collections agent, who will be able to pursue the matter face to face, and will again have experience in the inevitable difficult conversations.

In some cases, these agents will not need to be authorised by the FCA, but more often than not they will be, and their activities will be suitably constrained as a result. Part of the reason for this is that, as explained elsewhere, ancillary credit-related regulated activities such as debt collection (but not pure vehicle repossession) extend to cover any activity involving an 'individual' (as defined by the 1974 Act to include small partnerships and unincorporated associations), regardless of whether the relevant agreement was or was not regulated. In practice, therefore, any organisation engaging in collections activity within the motor vehicle finance market (either as a primary activity, or as an adjunct to repossession work) is likely to be an authorised firm, with its activities subject to oversight by the FCA. Even if this is not the case, however, the majority of motor vehicle Finance Companies are themselves regulated by the FCA. Overall, therefore, this area of the industry is generally either directly or indirectly regulated. On the other hand, there are still clear distinctions to be drawn between the recovery of vehicles and/or debts which are subject to a regulated agreement, as compared to those which are not. As with so many other areas of motor vehicle finance law, there are additional protections to consider in connection with the former.

The first point to remember in this regard is that repossession and debt collection agents are just that; agents of the Finance Company. Accordingly, the Finance Company is responsible for their actions, and is therefore under a pro-active responsibility to ensure that they carry out their instructions in an appropriate fashion. Accordingly, the relevant restrictions in this area apply primarily to the Finance Companies; the liability of the agents themselves is secondary.

Perhaps the most basic protection in the context of motor vehicle finance is the status of 'Protected Goods', as set out in section 90. This only applies to hire purchase and conditional sale agreements; in particular, it has no relevance whatsoever to hire agreements. However, where it does apply and the Customer has paid more than one-third of the total payable under the agreement (including any deposit or other advance), the Finance Company is unable to recover the vehicle without a court order. The 1974 Act says that section 90 does not apply if the debtor exercises their right to VT under section 99; otherwise the restriction in section 90 is absolute.

At least it would appear from the wording of section 90 itself to be absolute; in fact the position is more subtle. Section 173, which outlaws any attempt to contract out of the provisions of the 1974 Act, also says that whenever anything can be done only on a court order, it can actually also be done with the consent of the Customer. Such consent needs to be genuine; in other words, truly voluntary, informed, and contemporaneous. However, if the Customer does consent to the Finance Company taking back the motor vehicle despite its status as Protected Goods, the Finance Company will have done nothing wrong.

There are reasons why the Customer may give such consent. Not doing so only delays the evil day, because the Finance Company will almost certainly just apply to obtain a delivery up order from the court. Such orders are often suspended on terms for payment by the Customer, but if the Customer can't in reality keep up sensible payments, refusal to hand the vehicle over on first request will only delay the inevitable. More than that, it is likely to increase the amount that the Customer will be liable to pay in the long run. This is partly because of the costs involved in the making of the court application, but also because the longer the sale of the vehicle by the Finance Company is delayed, the lower the net proceeds are likely to be, and the less credit the Customer will get against the balance outstanding on the agreement.

Of course, as stated above, it is important that the Customer's consent is genuine. Accordingly, in order to guarantee that Finance Companies ensure that neither they, nor any agents acting on their behalf, overstep the mark, section 91 makes a breach of section 90 particularly punitive. Not only is the Customer released from all further liability under the agreement, but they are also entitled to get back from the Finance Company all sums that have been paid to date. In other words, if the Finance Company does overstep the mark, it may be able to get its hands on the net proceeds of sale of a second-hand vehicle, but will lose everything else.

In the circumstances, Finance Companies have a particular interest in making Customer's consent clear. This is done through a process which is usually referred to as 'voluntary surrender' or VS. In the same way as sections 99 and 100 are often referred to as the 'one half rule', sections 90 and 91 are often referred to as the 'one third rule'. Perhaps it is the similarity of expression, or the use of the word 'voluntary' in connection with both rules, but there is an unfortunate tendency to confuse voluntary surrender and voluntary termination, despite the fact that the two have no real connection whatsoever. 'VT' is the right of the Customer to terminate the agreement early, in order to return the vehicle and limit their outstanding liability. By contrast, VS is the conscious giving up by the Customer of their right to hold onto the vehicle as Protected Goods, following a default termination by the Finance Company.

Be that as it may, the usual arrangement is for the Finance Company, or its agent, to present the Customer with a VS form, which explains the position, and which will need to be signed before the vehicle can be repossessed. However, if persuasion is unsuccessful and the Customer declines to sign, there is little more for the repossession agent to do but to withdraw gracefully.

This is particularly so, given that section 92 of the 1974 Act makes it a breach of statutory duty for a Finance Company (which in practice means its agent) to enter into any premises in order to take possession of goods which are subject to a regulated agreement, whether it be one of credit or hire. Again, the apparent simplicity of this provision is tempered by the fact that the Finance Company is able to do so with an order from the court, which means that section 173 again applies. As a result, the Finance Company or its agent may enter the premises to take possession with the genuine consent of the Customer. A repossession agent may therefore walk up the drive of the Customer's house in reliance on a deemed invitation to approach the front door, and will be able to recover the car if the Customer agrees to allow this to happen. However, if the Customer makes it clear that their presence is not welcome, the agent will need to withdraw.

Whilst they do also apply to business purpose regulated agreements, sections 90, 91 and 92 are really designed to protect consumers from forms of repossession activity which are otherwise perfectly legitimate. In particular, self-help or 'snatchback' arrangements are acceptable in general law as long as the agents do not overstep the general mark, because the Finance Company is only seeking to recover possession of its own property. However, because of these sections, such approaches are not in practice permissible in connection with any regulated motor vehicle finance agreement.

As previously mentioned, if a Finance Company is unable to recover a vehicle, it may well apply to the court for an order requiring it to be delivered up. Under section 141, the County Court has exclusive jurisdiction in respect of all actions which involve the enforcement of an agreement regulated by the 1974 Act. Accordingly, the application for a delivery up order will be made to a County Court judge. The Customer will have an opportunity to put in a defence, but in most cases the only real question is whether the order should be effective immediately, or suspended if and for so long as the Customer complies with terms set out by the court.

In setting these terms, a judge is required to balance the interests of the Finance Company against those of the Customer. This means that (in theory at least) the terms should be based on reasonable evidence that the Customer can afford to make the promised payments, and provide for such payments to discharge the agreement or bring it back up to date within a reasonable period. If the Customer is not able to put forward such proposals, or if a suspended order is made but the terms are subsequently breached by the Customer, the Finance Company will be entitled to take possession; if necessary, with the assistance of a County Court bailiff.

Whether or not an order for delivery up is required, applications can also be made in respect of the shortfall due under a terminated agreement. Of course, such applications are a commercial process and will only be made by a Finance Company if there is a reasonable prospect that the costs involved can be justified by the likelihood of recovery.

Lastly, the court does have a number of extended powers under the terms of the 1974 Act. Most of these date back to the original drafting, and are intended to supplement the primary orders that the court can make. In respect to an application for an enforcement order, section 127 states that it should be dismissed 'if, but only if' the court thinks it just to do so having regard to:

- prejudice caused to any person (usually, but not necessarily the Customer);
- the Finance Company's culpability for the breach; and
- the court's powers under the 1974 Act to vary the terms of the agreement and/or impose conditions on the enforcement order.

In practice, therefore, the two major questions to answer are whether the customer has suffered any detriment for which the Court cannot compensate by the exercise of its supplemental powers, and whether the court thinks that the Finance Company's actions were so deliberate or unreasonable as to justify a refusal to allow enforcement.

As regards those supplementary powers, these include:

- Section 133 which allows for the return, or even the transfer, of the vehicle to the Customer; and

- Sections 135 and 136 which give the court powers to impose conditions on, suspend the operation of, or vary the terms of, any order it makes.

Of rather wider application, though, is section 140A; usually referred to as the 'unfair relationships' provision. This has no application to hire agreements, but does apply to any credit agreement entered into by an 'individual' (as defined by the 1974 Act), whether regulated or unregulated.

As originally designed, the 1974 Act contained a provision allowing the court to intervene if a credit agreement amounted to an 'extortionate credit bargain'. However, this proved to be a difficult concept to enforce, engendering much technical argument about what was or was not an ECB. As a result, the 2006 Act did away with the concept and replaced it with that of the 'unfair relationship'. The provisions are drafted particularly widely in order to give the court maximum discretion when deciding when a relationship was unfair, and what it should do about it.

Broadly, the court is able to make an order if it finds that the relationship between the Finance Company and the Customer is 'unfair' by reason of:

- The terms of the agreement, or any related agreement;

- The way that the Finance Company has exercised its rights; or

- Anything done or not done, by or on behalf of the Finance Company, whether before or after the making of the agreement.

As will be appreciated, this is all extremely wide and there is (deliberately) no attempt to define what constitutes unfairness. It is also the case that it is up to the Finance Company to prove that the relationship was fair, rather than for the Customer to prove that it was unfair. The Customer does have to go some way beyond making a bare and unsupported allegation. However, if a potential basis for the allegation of unfairness has been identified by the Customer, the onus is then on the Finance Company to prove otherwise. If the Finance Company fails to do so, the court's powers are almost unlimited, provided that they are directed towards remedying the unfairness in the relationship that has been identified.

Finally, some limited consideration of collections activity. The FCA Handbook contains much detail on how this area of a Finance Companies affairs should be conducted. Most of that detail tends to focus on the extremes of collections activity, and is outside the focus of this book. However, there are some important general points to be made on the subject.

The central concept of 'forbearance' has already been mentioned, and any authorised firm will need to strike a fair balance between its own interests and those of its defaulting Customers whenever it is seeking the payment of arrears or a post termination shortfall. This will, in itself, involve consideration of the equally central concept of 'affordability'; can the defaulting Customer afford to make a particular level of repayment without it impacting adversely on their financial circumstances? More than this, such activity is bound to involve Customers who are, for a variety of reasons, 'vulnerable'. Indeed, it can be argued that a defaulting Customer is by definition vulnerable.

As such, Finance Companies need to have detailed policies and processes in place to ensure that all collections activity, whether carried out in-house or through external agents, is proactively controlled in order to ensure that these central concepts are given due regard at all times. This is of course particularly true in respect of a consumer customer, but even business customers must be treated appropriately. As ever, the context is essential, and there is scope for different approaches to be adopted in respect of 'business' and 'consumer' debt. However, it should always be remembered that sole traders, partners and guarantors are all individuals, and that whilst it may be acceptable to adopt a certain approach when dealing with 'the business', that does not mean that the same approach will be acceptable once the business is gone, and it is only the individual who is left to pick up the tab from their own resources. In such cases, the quondam business debt must be seen as a 'consumer' collection activity.

In many, if not most, cases, the use of court action as a collection activity will be unnecessary or pointless. Such procedures are expensive, and if the Customer cannot pay the debt, what is the point of obtaining a piece of paper requiring them to do so? That said, such action is sometimes necessary. In general, claims will be brought in the County Court (indeed, if the agreement was regulated, only the County Court has jurisdiction). The Finance Company will tend to take such action if it considers that the expense of doing so can be commercially justified because there is a genuine prospect of recovery. In many cases, this will be because the Customer is the owner of property in respect of which a Charging Order can be obtained in order to secure the judgment debt.

None of this is particularly limited to motor vehicle finance. However, mention should be made of one last information requirement that applies in respect of any judgment based on a regulated agreement which provides for default interest to be payable at a contract rate after that judgment has been entered.

It is standard practice for motor finance agreements to provide that default interest will be paid on sums that are overdue. The default rate needs to be reasonable; if it is too high, it could be struck out as being a penalty. However, in general law, as long as the rate is reasonable, the defaulting party will be liable to pay the additional interest as well as the overdue sum.

There is a twist in respect of a regulated agreement, because the 1974 Act prevents default interest being charged at a rate higher than that which was used to calculate the credit charges. So, for example, if the regulated agreement were 0% APR, no default interest can be charged at all. For this reason, whilst it is commonplace for unregulated agreements to state a specific default rate applicable in all cases, the default interest term in a regulated agreement will instead link to the inherent interest rate for the particular transaction, as stated on the face of the agreement.

It is also important in respect of regulated transactions to remember that, technically, when a court judgment is entered in respect of a debt, the debt itself ceases to exist. The sum in question is no longer owed under the contract; it is owed under the judgment. Most judgment debts, whether in the High Court or the County Court, automatically carry statutory interest. Generally, therefore, Finance Companies are able to obtain contractual interest on overdue sums up to the point of judgment, and will then be entitled to statutory interest thereafter.

However, whilst this is fine for unregulated transactions, the situation is more complicated for regulated agreements. Although not as often appreciated as it should be, court judgments based on a regulated agreement do not accrue statutory interest. This is deliberate. However, whilst many Finance Companies simply regard this as being a fact of life in the regulated sector, there is an alternative for those which wish to continue charging interest after the entry of a judgment. It is possible for any contract (regulated or unregulated) to provide that contractual interest will continue to accrue even after a judgment has been entered. There is a special process required to ensure that the judgment is entered in the right form so as to allow this to happen, but if this is followed, contractual interest continues to accrue even on a regulated agreement.

This was long seen by the OFT as being an unfair practice. The OFT was unsuccessful in having the practice outlawed through the courts, but as a fall-back arranged for the 2006 Act to include a provision which would require Finance Companies wishing to engage in this practice to give specific notice to the Customer affected.

In simple terms, a Finance Company wishing to avail itself of post-judgment interest will need to give the Customer notice of this after the judgment has been entered. It is not entitled to charge that interest until it has given the notice; furthermore, it cannot continue charging the interest thereafter unless it gives further notices, reminding the Customer, at not more than six-monthly intervals.

Again, the notice is really intended to be for information purposes. It is intended to ensure that the Customer is aware of the issue, and can (in theory at least) do something about it. For the same reasons, where a regulated agreement contains a provision allowing for post-judgment interest, the Finance Company is required to include an extra paragraph in any Default Notice explaining the position, whether or not it actually invokes the clause in practice.

MORE BOOKS BY LAW BRIEF PUBLISHING

A selection of our other titles available now:-

'A Practical Guide to Vicarious Liability' by Mariel Irvine
'A Practical Guide to Claims Arising from Delays in Diagnosing Cancer' by Bella Webb
'A Practical Guide to Applications for Landlord's Consent and Variation of Leases' by Mark Shelton
'A Practical Guide to Relief from Sanctions Post-Mitchell and Denton' by Peter Causton
'Butler's Equine Tax Planning: 2nd Edition' by Julie Butler
'A Practical Guide to Equity Release for Advisors' by Paul Sams
'A Practical Guide to Immigration Law and Tier 1 Entrepreneur Applications' by Sarah Pinder
'A Practical Guide to Unlawful Eviction and Harassment' by Stephanie Lovegrove
'In My Backyard! A Practical Guide to Neighbourhood Plans' by Dr Sue Chadwick
'A Practical Guide to the Law Relating to Food' by Ian Thomas
'A Practical Guide to the Ending of Assured Shorthold Tenancies' by Elizabeth Dwomoh
'Commercial Mediation – A Practical Guide' by Nick Carr
'A Practical Guide to Financial Services Claims' by Chris Hegarty
'The Law of Houses in Multiple Occupation: A Practical Guide to HMO Proceedings' by Julian Hunt
'A Practical Guide to Unlawful Eviction and Harassment' by Stephanie Lovegrove
'A Practical Guide to Solicitor and Client Costs' by Robin Dunne
'Artificial Intelligence – The Practical Legal Issues' by John Buyers
'A Practical Guide to Wrongful Conception, Wrongful Birth and Wrongful Life Claims' by Rebecca Greenstreet

‘Occupiers, Highways and Defective Premises Claims: A Practical Guide Post-Jackson – 2nd Edition’ by Andrew Mckie

‘A Practical Guide to Financial Ombudsman Service Claims’ by Adam Temple & Robert Scrivenor

‘A Practical Guide to the Law of Enfranchisement and Lease Extension’ by Paul Sams

‘A Practical Guide to Marketing for Lawyers – 2nd Edition’ by Catherine Bailey & Jennet Ingram

'A Practical Guide to Advising Schools on Employment Law' by Jonathan Holden

'Certificates of Lawful Use and Development: A Guide to Making and Determining Applications' by Bob Mc Geady & Meyric Lewis

'A Practical Guide to the Law of Dilapidations' by Mark Shelton

‘A Practical Guide to the 2018 Jackson Personal Injury and Costs Reforms’ by Andrew Mckie

‘A Guide to Consent in Clinical Negligence Post-Montgomery’ by Lauren Sutherland QC

‘A Practical Guide to Running Housing Disrepair and Cavity Wall Claims: 2nd Edition’ by Andrew Mckie & Ian Skeate

‘A Practical Guide to the General Data Protection Regulation (GDPR)’ by Keith Markham

‘A Practical Guide to Digital and Social Media Law for Lawyers’ by Sherree Westell

‘A Practical Guide to Holiday Sickness Claims – 2nd Edition’ by Andrew Mckie & Ian Skeate

‘A Practical Guide to Inheritance Act Claims by Adult Children Post-Ilott v Blue Cross’ by Sheila Hamilton Macdonald

‘A Practical Guide to Elderly Law’ by Justin Patten

‘Arguments and Tactics for Personal Injury and Clinical Negligence Claims’ by Dorian Williams

‘A Practical Guide to QOCS and Fundamental Dishonesty’ by James Bentley

‘A Practical Guide to Drone Law’ by Rufus Ballaster, Andrew Firman, Eleanor Clot

‘Practical Mediation: A Guide for Mediators, Advocates, Advisers, Lawyers, and Students in Civil, Commercial, Business, Property, Workplace, and Employment Cases’ by Jonathan Dingle with John Sephton

'Practical Horse Law: A Guide for Owners and Riders' by Brenda Gilligan
'A Comparative Guide to Standard Form Construction and Engineering Contracts' by Jon Close
'A Practical Guide to Compliance for Personal Injury Firms Working With Claims Management Companies' by Paul Bennett
'A Practical Guide to the Landlord and Tenant Act 1954: Commercial Tenancies' by Richard Hayes & David Sawtell
'A Practical Guide to Personal Injury Claims Involving Animals' by Jonathan Hand
'A Practical Guide to Psychiatric Claims in Personal Injury' by Liam Ryan
'Introduction to the Law of Community Care in England and Wales' by Alan Robinson
'A Practical Guide to Dog Law for Owners and Others' by Andrea Pitt
'Ellis and Kevan on Credit Hire – 5th Edition' by Aidan Ellis & Tim Kevan
'RTA Allegations of Fraud in a Post-Jackson Era: The Handbook – 2nd Edition' by Andrew Mckie
'RTA Personal Injury Claims: A Practical Guide Post-Jackson' by Andrew Mckie
'On Experts: CPR35 for Lawyers and Experts' by David Boyle
'An Introduction to Personal Injury Law' by David Boyle
'A Practical Guide to Claims Arising From Accidents Abroad and Travel Claims' by Andrew Mckie & Ian Skeate
'A Practical Guide to Cosmetic Surgery Claims' by Dr Victoria Handley
'A Practical Guide to Chronic Pain Claims' by Pankaj Madan
'A Practical Guide to Claims Arising from Fatal Accidents' by James Patience
'A Practical Approach to Clinical Negligence Post-Jackson' by Geoffrey Simpson-Scott
'A Practical Guide to Personal Injury Trusts' by Alan Robinson
'Employers' Liability Claims: A Practical Guide Post-Jackson' by Andrew Mckie
'A Practical Guide to Subtle Brain Injury Claims' by Pankaj Madan
'The Law of Driverless Cars: An Introduction' by Alex Glassbrook
'A Practical Guide to Costs in Personal Injury Cases' by Matthew Hoe

'A Practical Guide to Alternative Dispute Resolution in Personal Injury Claims – Getting the Most Out of ADR Post-Jackson' by Peter Causton, Nichola Evans, James Arrowsmith
'A Practical Guide to Personal Injuries in Sport' by Adam Walker & Patricia Leonard
'The No Nonsense Solicitors' Practice: A Guide To Running Your Firm' by Bettina Brueggemann
'Baby Steps: A Guide to Maternity Leave and Maternity Pay' by Leah Waller
'The Queen's Counsel Lawyer's Omnibus: 20 Years of Cartoons from The Times 1993-2013' by Alex Steuart Williams

These books and more are available to order online direct from the publisher at www.lawbriefpublishing.com, where you can also read free sample chapters. For any queries, contact us on 0844 587 2383 or mail@lawbriefpublishing.com.

Our books are also usually in stock at www.amazon.co.uk with free next day delivery for Prime members, and at good legal bookshops such as Hammicks and Wildy & Sons.

We are regularly launching new books in our series of practical day-to-day practitioners' guides. Visit our website and join our free newsletter to be kept informed and to receive special offers, free chapters, etc.

You can also follow us on Twitter at www.twitter.com/lawbriefpub.

www.ingramcontent.com/pod-product-compliance
Lightning Source LLC
LaVergne TN
LVHW022048200926
848481LV00003B/829
9781912687008